THE YOUNG CHURCHILL

THE YOUNG CHURCHILL

The Early Years of Winston Churchill

Celia Sandys

A WILLIAM ABRAHAMS BOOK

DUTTON

DUTTON
Published by the Penguin Group
Penguin Books USA Inc., 375 Hudson Street, New York, New York 10014, U.S.A.
Penguin Books Ltd, 27 Wrights Lane, London W8 5TZ, England
Penguin Books Australia Ltd, Ringwood, Victoria, Australia
Penguin Books Canada Ltd, 10 Alcorn Avenue, Toronto, Ontario, Canada M4V 3B2
Penguin Books (N.Z.) Ltd, 182–190 Wairau Road, Auckland 10, New Zealand

Penguin Books Ltd, Registered Offices: Harmondsworth, Middlesex, England

Published by Dutton, an imprint of Dutton Signet, a division of Penguin Books USA Inc.
Previously published in Great Britain by Sinclair-Stevenson as *From Winston with Love and Kisses*

First Dutton Printing, September, 1995
10 9 8 7 6 5 4 3 2 1

The author and publisher are grateful to Curtis Brown Ltd, London to reproduce material on behalf of

The Estate of Sir Winston S. Churchill: for the use of material from *My Early Life* © The Estate of Sir Winston
S. Churchill 1930; for the use of material from *Painting as a Pastime* © The Estate of Sir Winston S. Churchill 1948;
and for the use of previously unpublished material © The Estate of Sir Winston S. Churchill 1994

C & T Publications: for the use of material from the Official Biography and Companion Volumes
© C & T Publications

Winston S. Churchill M.P.: for the reproduction of photographs from The Broadwater Collection

Churchill Heritage Ltd: for the reproduction of the Paintings of Sir Winston S. Churchill © Churchill Heritage Ltd

REGISTERED TRADEMARK—MARCA REGISTRADA

LIBRARY OF CONGRESS CATALOGING-IN-PUBLICATION DATA
Sandys, Celia.
    [From Winston with love and kisses]
    The young Churchill : the early years of Winston Churchill / by Celia Sandys.
        p.   cm.
    "A William Abrahams book."
    "Previously published in Great Britain by Sinclair-Stevenson as
From Winston with love and kisses"—T.p. verso.
    ISBN 0-525-94048-0
    1. Churchill, Winston, Sir, 1874–1965—Childhood and youth.
    2. Prime ministers—Great Britain—Bibliography.   I. Title.
DA566.9.C5C26   1995
941.084'092—dc20   95–30277
[B]   CIP

Printed in the United States of America

This book is printed on acid-free paper. ∞

Half-title: Winston's first haircut
Frontispiece: Winston in Dublin aged 4

This book is lovingly dedicated to
Justin, Dominic, Alexander and Sophie

ACKNOWLEDGEMENTS

I wish first to acknowledge my gratitude to Her Majesty The Queen for her gracious permission to reproduce the painting by my grandfather of the Palladian Bridge at Wilton.

I wish to thank: the Duke of Marlborough for permission to photograph and reproduce material in his possession and Paul Duffie, the chief administrator at Blenheim Palace, for all his help; the Keepers and Governors of Harrow School for their kind permission to photograph and reproduce material, Dale Vargas, housemaster of the Headmaster's House, for his help, and most particularly the school archivist, Alsadair Hawkyard, for his patient and enthusiastic assistance in my search through the archives; Alan Kucia and Moira MacKay at the Churchill Archives Centre for their help; The Commandant, Royal Military Academy Sandhurst, for permission to reproduce material and Martine de Lee, the assistant curator at Sandhurst; Jo Brennan, Deputy Secretary to the President of the Republic of Ireland; the National Trust for permission to reproduce pictures in their possession and the administrator of Chartwell, Jean Broome, for her help; Anthea Griggs, the headmistress of St George's School, Ascot for her willing and invaluable assistance; Mr and Mrs F. Bartlett Watt for allowing me to reproduce material in their possession.

I would like to express my gratitude to the following who have all helped in a variety of ways: the Reverend Richard Capstick; Dr James Carleton Paget; Noel and June Chanan; Gary Clark; Robert Hardy; Josephine Izzett; Richard Langworth; Dr John H. Mather; Nicolas Thompson and Wylma Wayne; Charles Hopkinson who has been responsible for most of the photographs and Craig Dodd who has taken so much care in the design of the book.

I am extremely grateful to Curtis Brown, and in particular to Anthea Morton-Saner, for help over copyright material.

I would like to thank everyone at Sinclair-Stevenson for their enthusiastic help and support. Most particularly my gratitude goes to my publisher and editor, Christopher Sinclair-Stevenson, who, by his wise and sensitive advice, has been a real friend in this my first foray into the world of books.

Without the support of my family there would have been no book. They have all given me help and encouragement from the very beginning. I would like to thank my cousin Winston S. Churchill, MP, for his generosity in allowing me to reproduce material to which he owns the copyright; my aunt, Lady Soames, for allowing me to reproduce photographs from her collection and for her enthusiastic support; my sister, Edwina Sandys, for her unflagging encouragement and loyal support throughout; my brother, Julian Sandys, QC, for his assistance in translating passages from German; and my stepmother, Lady Duncan-Sandys, for her generous hospitality at all times.

Most especially my thanks go to my cousin Peregrine Churchill who has not only allowed me to use many letters and photographs from his personal collection but has also been my staunch ally, adviser and friendly critic from the beginning, and to his wife, Yvonne, who has put up with our constant discussions and whose pleasure at the completion of this book will only be tempered by the prospect of the commencement of the next.

Finally my heartfelt thanks to my husband, Ken Perkins, whose efficient and patient help and loving support has made it all possible.

CONTENTS

FOREWORD

If you know a lonely child who has poetry in its heart but a tongue distorting the words it tries to utter, whose muscles refuse to obey and fingers drop what it would grasp, whose infantile achievements wither from lack of encouragement; let it listen to the story of young Winston's boyhood and learn to believe there is always hope, and never, never give up.

When Winston was nearly eight years old, he was taken by his mother and left at boarding school, as was the custom in those days. He thus found himself suddenly translated into a bewildering and hostile society very different from home, at the modest little house No.2 St James's Place, with his baby brother and attentive nurse. He had relished the walks in the Green Park with his mother and the stories she would read to him at bedtime. He must have watched her draw and paint in the afternoons; but often he was bundled back to the nursery while important people from Parliament came to discuss affairs with his father.

This cosy little nursery was exchanged for a hard and sometimes cruel schooling system where first he had to learn how to survive against the ailments fickle Nature had unreasonably given him at birth; and then the tyranny of schoolmasters who would have him learn, with threat of the birch, subjects in which he had no interest or understanding. He wrote his first letters home, trying to hide his tears and bewilderment. Thus began a private and intimate correspondence between mother and son, which continued for forty years.

Winston was descended on both sides from notable families. Some ingredients of antecedents and environment must have influence on personality. His father, Lord Randolph, could speak fluent German, French and Latin. A cultured life would have been his choice but when duty, as a younger son of the Duke of Marlborough, forced him into politics, he made the best of it and once there his ability propelled him to the top in record time. Winston took great interest in his father's political progress very early in his schooldays. His letters in this book show a maturity well in advance of his age. He was longing to grow up and follow in his father's footsteps; he first devoted all his energy to overcome his physical disabilities. A speech impediment and other physical faults should have given a normal child little hope for a political career. But stamina inherited perhaps from his mother and grandmother, the seventh Duchess of Marlborough, overcame the natural process of nature.

His father, whom he greatly admired, died shortly before he came of age. Winston, after ten years of boarding schools which he hated, had left with his education incomplete. It would seem he should never have been sent to a public school but it is idle to conjecture what might have been. It was unfortunate he never learnt from or understood his father while alive.

Winston's mother, Jennie Jerome, was my grandmother and the most wonderful grandmother anyone could imagine. I met her first in the 1914 War. She was always known as BM (Belle Mere); her father's family had emigrated from England and her mother's family was supposed to have Iroquois Indian ancestry not so far in the past.

Certainly Jennie's striking beauty had some of the dark features of the North American Indian race. One of her aunts was known as Battle Axe by the nephews. Her father had wanted a boy so she was allowed to wear trousers and ride astride, becoming a magnificent horsewoman; he also started the New York Opera, and Jennie's talents made her a remarkable concert pianist. Mr Jerome had the misfortune to be on the wrong side in the American Civil War, so it was convenient to move to Europe for two years. Mrs Jerome was so attracted by European culture that she returned with her three

Peregrine Churchill with Lady Randolph

daughters and settled in Paris. Jennie found a new life and decided to be French. She changed her name to Jeannette and put accents on all the vowels in Jerome.

Jennie had the ability of making you feel on equal terms whoever you were. When I was four years old I had no nurse and my mother had to take me with her and once, at a party with BM, I had slipped away, found a piano and was playing the scales on the black notes. My mother shouted for me to stop but BM left the party and, sitting beside me, told me I had played the Siegfried motif. She then recited the whole Wagner story, playing the various parts. I remember particularly her explaining that the birds singing in the trees were really only fat old sopranos. Her guests were left to entertain themselves. My love for music started at that point.

I was often left to stay at her London house, looked after by her maid and the cook. In those days a lady could never go out alone in London, she must have a male escort; there were usually plenty of men willing to oblige. She asked me to escort her on occasions and I took her once to the American Hospital near Paddington, which she had organised. I was encouraged to talk to the wounded; looking back, I realise some of the wounds were horrific but at the time I was just curious. Jennie spoke to everyone and in a few minutes the ward was full of smiling and laughing faces. I was four-and-a-half years old at that time and could not open the taxi door; to my annoyance a grown up Scout, at least twelve, did it for me. I am often accused that my impressions of childhood are exaggerated, but in this case, recently going through the Archives at Churchill College, I found a photograph, and there was the Hospital and Taxi and the Boy Scout.

Everything was always easy and interesting with Granny BM. She had a natural artistic temperament, it is sad her many paintings have never been found; I have her rough sketch for her book plate, two cherubs playing a lyre, and a bar of music she composed for a motto. Everything was top quality and later she made a business decorating houses. It was not until much later, when I became Executor for her estate, after my father, that I realised how low her income had become. There is little doubt about her excellent taste; her furniture from her small house was auctioned in 1921 for £70,000, which was a lot of money in those days. The auction catalogue reads like a guide to the Victoria and Albert Museum. The sum paid off the Bank overdraft; Rothschild had backed her credit, who else would know her worth better?

Sir Winston's granddaughter, Celia Sandys, has devoted four years tracing lost letters and selecting the best

from a thousand or more, for the limited space available for publication. She has travelled all over this country and Europe tracking down the routes and houses Winston knew, finding some locations hardly changed and even interesting evidence of his presence in some of the unspoilt places.

No one without Celia's energy could have done this task. No need to enquire from where the energy came. Thanks are due to the forefathers of the dark beauty Jennie Jerome and the seventh Duchess of Marlborough through the royal Stuarts and the Villiers connection. Strangely enough, the early Churchills were also connected with the first Villiers through the West Country Drakes. There lies the heart of England that made this country Great and begat the English-speaking world.

Peregrine S. Churchill

Trustee of the Churchill Archives and last surviving link with Sir Winston Churchill's mother, Lady Randolph Churchill.

INTRODUCTION

If the child born at Blenheim Palace a hundred and twenty years ago had not, against all the odds, survived his early years, the world we live in today would be a very different place.

Many books have been written about Winston Churchill. They have covered his public life from all angles. His years of despair in the political wilderness and his triumph as wartime Prime Minister have been chronicled, praised and criticised. Apart from his own brief account in *My Early Life*, all these books, containing millions of words and diverse opinions, have one thing in common: they pay scant attention to his formative years and to the influences of childhood which contributed to the character of the man who was destined to lead his country in its darkest hour.

How fortunate for me to have the privilege to step into the vacuum left by others and to have the opportunity to journey through the early life of the grandfather I knew only in his later years.

Anyone who lived through the Second World War remembers Winston Churchill. The generation of War Babies, to which I belong, remembers his funeral. Now, however, there is a new generation to whom Churchill is only a name in the pages of history like Nelson and Wellington, Napoleon and Julius Caesar. While there are still people living who were inspired by his speeches, knew him, worked with him, just shook his hand, queued for hours in the freezing cold to pay their last respects, or simply loved him, he cannot rest on a dusty bookshelf. I hope, in these pages, to bring to life the early years of the impish, lonely and sickly little boy who, by his own tenacious attitude to life, lived to fulfil his youthful dreams and fantasies.

For over a century the private writings of the young Winston have been preserved and more or less ignored: his first smudgy mark, childish letters, schoolboy letters, happy letters, sad letters, proud letters, pleading letters, letters of apology and even the pitiful letter which, but for the devoted care of his doctor, would have been the last letter he ever wrote. His mother kept them all, together with his first artistic efforts and his school reports. Some schoolmasters spotted merit in his work and saved for posterity essays and verse written by the boy whose legendary academic ineptitude has been a comfort to many parents of "late developers".

I grew up in the aftermath of the Second World War at a time when Winston Churchill was an object of respect and adoration in the eyes of the British Public even though they had just voted him out of office. This unexpected outcome of the General Election of 1945 left my grandparents without a London home and it was to my parents' Westminster flat, where I had been born as the bombs fell on London some two years earlier, that they moved.

We, my brother Julian, my sister Edwina and I, lived with our mother and father nearby and grew up more or less unaware of the fame of our grandfather. The first time I remember feeling in any way different from other children was when King George VI died and my grandfather was once more Prime Minister. Edwina and I were sent to school protesting madly at the black crêpe bands we had been told we must wear on the sleeves of our grey tweed coats. We could not understand why, as our Nanny put it, "We, as the grandchildren of the Prime Minister, must show respect." We may not have been the only respectful children but we certainly felt we were and I remember being teased unmercifully and being unable to give my friends the reason for fear of being accused of boasting or worse still lying.

For most of our childhood we did not have a country house and money was short so it was to our grandparents at Chequers and Chartwell that we children were sent for our holidays. My grandmother organised the best Christmases I have ever known. The whole family gathered together and for the children it was certainly a magical time which has spoilt me for Christmas ever since.

An aspect of life into which I was introduced by my grandfather was the world of grand hotels and foreign travel. My first experience in an hotel was with my grandfather at the Hotel de Paris in Monte Carlo. I was fifteen at the time and having been escorted from the airport by a troop of police outriders we arrived at the hotel where I was shown to the grandest bedroom I had ever seen. My clothes were unpacked, my bath run, and there always seemed to be someone longing to do something for me. I quite naturally assumed that this was what hotels were all about. I decided that I would like to spend a lot of time being pampered in this way in the future. Not surprisingly hotels however good have never come up to my early experiences. These were holidays which I would not have missed for anything. They gave me the chance to feel close to the grandfather whom everyone thought they owned. We would go for drives, I would watch him painting or we would just sit together on the terrace while the sun went down over the Mediterranean. One thing he had not forgotten even when very old – young people are always short of money. He certainly could never get enough of it when he was young, so his last question before I left was always, "Are you all right for money?" as he thrust a wad of notes, perhaps won at the Casino the night before, into my hand.

This man who had been such an inspiration to his country and who had led such a tumultuous life was in his final years a very peaceful person to be with. He liked above all to be at Chartwell where, accompanied by his beloved Clementine, one of his children or an available grandchild, he could pursue the undemanding pleasures of feeding the goldfish or visiting the black swans on the lake that he had himself created. We were all willing companions knowing only too well that time was running out. On his seventy-fifth birthday he had said: "I am ready to meet my Maker. Whether my Maker is prepared for the great ordeal of meeting me is another matter." Ready he undoubtedly was but in his own mind the time had not arrived for he had predicted that he would die on the same day as his father. And so it was that on the seventieth anniversary of Lord Randolph's death he finally slipped away for the meeting to which he had referred fifteen years before. Family good-byes having been said, the machinery of State took over and the British people, in whom he had had so much faith, made sure that their hero had the best possible send-off on his final journey.

This pilgrimage has taken me down many contradictory paths and caused me to ask many questions. Was he neglected by his parents? Was he really so stupid at school? How could this child, unless blessed with nine lives, have overcome his congenital weaknesses and survived so many hair-raising accidents and heroic escapades to live beyond his ninetieth birthday?

What guardian angel watched over the boy who was to take part in the last great cavalry charge, be captured by the Boers, escape and have a price put on his head, enter Parliament at the age of twenty-five and there serve six monarchs, fight in the trenches, be twice Prime Minister, write forty-four books and receive the Nobel Prize for Literature, paint more than five hundred pictures and be made an Honorary Royal Academician, become a Knight of the Garter, an Honorary Citizen of the United States of America, and be honoured, decorated and revered in all corners of the earth?

Mine has been a delightful and sentimental voyage of discovery, at times happy, at times sad but always fascinating. Around every corner I have found something new, spurring me on to find out more about this extraordinary man whom I am proud to have called Grandpapa.

Note. I have reproduced letters and essays as they were originally written, including misspellings, the inconsistent use of capitals and random punctuation. Winston's own words are printed in bold type.

CHRONOLOGY

1874 Winston Churchill born at Blenheim on 30th November.
1877 Lord and Lady Randolph and Winston go to Ireland.
1878 Winston concussed in fall from donkey.
1880 Winston's brother Jack born on 4th February. The Churchill family return to London.
1882 Winston's first letter. Holidays at Blenheim. Learns to ride. Goes to St George's School, Ascot.
1883 Feuds with authority, kicks headmaster's straw hat to pieces.
1884 Removed from St George's and sent to school at Brighton. Lady Randolph cannot control Winston. Winston stabbed.
1885 Poor health.
1886 Nearly dies of pneumonia. Top of school in gymnastics.
1887 First step in politics, joins Primrose League. Attends Queen Victoria's Jubilee celebrations. The Prince of Wales is impressed.
1888 Enters Harrow. Joins school Rifle Corps. Wins prize for reciting 1,200 lines of Macaulay.
1889 Concussed in fall from bicycle. Joins Army Class. Takes up fencing.
1890 Wins prize for poetry. Gives up smoking. Passes Preliminary Examination for Sandhurst.

1891 Considers joining the Church. Mrs Everest sends Winston heroin. Flogged for breaking windows. Rebels against spending holidays with French family. Decides to buy a bulldog.
1892 Becomes public schools fencing champion. July, takes entrance examination to Sandhurst Military Academy and fails. November, fails his second attempt to enter Sandhurst. Leaves Harrow.
1893 Seriously injured in fall from tree. Passes Sandhurst examination at third attempt. Narrowly escapes drowning in Switzerland. Enters Sandhurst as cadet for the 60th Rifles. Promises Lord Randolph he will restrict cigars to one or two a day.
1894 Agitates to join Cavalry. Loses watch. Head of riding class. First publication in national press. First public speech. Passes out of Sandhurst 20th out of 130.
1895 Lord Randolph dies. Mrs Everest dies. Winston commissioned into the 4th Hussars.

WINSTON'S FAMILY TREE

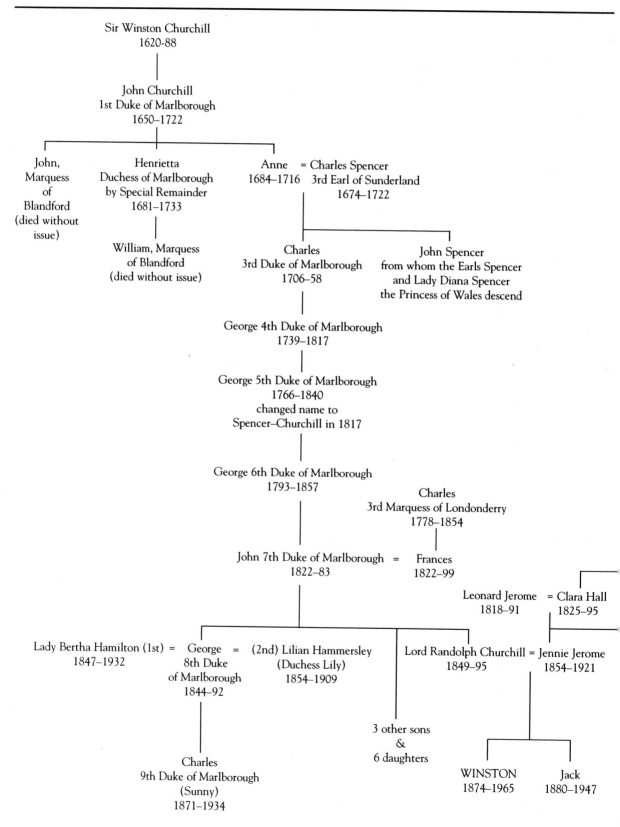

Sir Winston Churchill
1620-88

John Churchill
1st Duke of Marlborough
1650–1722

John,
Marquess
of
Blandford
(died without
issue)

Henrietta
Duchess of Marlborough
by Special Remainder
1681–1733

William, Marquess
of Blandford
(died without issue)

Anne = Charles Spencer
1684–1716 3rd Earl of Sunderland
1674–1722

Charles
3rd Duke of Marlborough
1706–58

John Spencer
from whom the Earls Spencer
and Lady Diana Spencer
the Princess of Wales descend

George 4th Duke of Marlborough
1739–1817

George 5th Duke of Marlborough
1766–1840
changed name to
Spencer–Churchill in 1817

George 6th Duke of Marlborough
1793–1857

Charles
3rd Marquess of Londonderry
1778–1854

John 7th Duke of Marlborough = Frances
1822–83   1822–99

Leonard Jerome = Clara Hall
1818–91   1825–95

Lady Bertha Hamilton (1st) = George = (2nd) Lilian Hammersley
1847–1932   8th Duke   (Duchess Lily)
                              of Marlborough 1854–1909
                              1844–92

Lord Randolph Churchill = Jennie Jerome
1849–95   1854–1921

3 other sons
&
6 daughters

Charles
9th Duke of Marlborough
(Sunny)
1871–1934

WINSTON
1874–1965

Jack
1880–1947

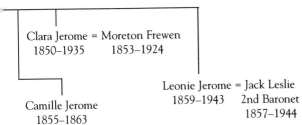

David Wilcox=Iroquois Indian

Clarissa Wilcox = Ambrose Hall
c1800–1827   1774–c1827

Clara Jerome = Moreton Frewen
1850–1935   1853–1924

Camille Jerome
1855–1863

Leonie Jerome = Jack Leslie
1859–1943   2nd Baronet
                      1857–1944

Above: Sir Winston Churchill, father of the 1st Duke

BIRTHS.

On the 30th Nov., at Blenheim Palace, the Lady RANDOLPH CHURCHILL, prematurely, of a son.

Winston Leonard Spencer Churchill was born at Blenheim Palace on 30th November 1874.

Queen Victoria had twenty-six more years to reign. Disraeli had that year displaced Gladstone as Prime Minister. The British Empire covered vast areas of the globe and every schoolchild's atlas was largely coloured red.

Europe was watching Bismarck preside over the rise of Germany, the menace of which was destined to play such a large part in the long life of this new baby.

America, with which he was always to feel a close affinity, was still struggling to nationhood in the aftermath of its Civil War.

This was a world of candles and gaslight, steam trains and horse-drawn vehicles, penny-farthings and Shanks's pony. The telephone, the electric light-bulb and the motor car had yet to be invented. Medicine was basic. There were no X-rays and no antibiotics; anaesthetics and antiseptics were still in the early stages of development.

Lord Randolph Churchill married Miss Jennie Jerome on 15th April 1874. Thirty-three weeks later, following a fall while she was walking with the guns, their first child was born. They had planned that the baby, expected the following January, would be born in their London home. Therefore, when Winston made his appearance several weeks ahead of time, nothing was prepared.

Lord Randolph wrote that same day to his mother-in-law, Mrs Leonard Jerome, who was in Paris.

Monday 30   Blenheim Palace
12.30 p.m.   Woodstock

Dear Mrs Jerome,

I have just time to write a line, to send by the London Dr to tell you that all has up to now thank God gone off very well with my darling Jennie. She had a fall on Tuesday walking with the shooters, & a rather imprudent & rough drive in a pony carriage brought on the pains on Saturday night. We tried to stop them, but it was no use. They went on all Sunday. Of course the Oxford physician cld not come. We telegraphed for the London man Dr Hope but he did not arrive till this morning. The country Dr is however a clever man, & the baby was safely born at 1.30 this morning after about 8 hrs labour. She suffered a good deal poor darling, but was vy plucky & had no chloroform. The boy is wonderfully pretty so everybody says dark eyes and hair & vy healthy considering its prematureness. My mother & Clementine have been everything to Jennie, & she cld not be more comfortable. We have just got a most excellent nurse & wet nurse coming down this afternoon, & please God all will go vy well with both. I telegraphed to Mr Jerome; I thought he wld like to hear. I am sure you will be delighted at this good news and dear Clara also I will write again tonight. Love to Clara

Yrs affty
Randolph S. C.

I hope the baby things will come with all speed. We have to borrow some from the Woodstock Solicitor's wife.

Opposite: Lady Randolph Churchill
Overleaf: Blenheim Palace

Lady Randolph had selected a fashionable London obstetrician to deliver her first child. Caught unawares by the premature birth of the baby, she was attended by the local doctor in a downstairs room while efforts were being made to replace him with a physician from Oxford pending the arrival of the celebrated London consultant.

Lord Randolph, while the Churchill women kept his wife company, had the endless corridors of Blenheim to pace in time-honoured fashion.

Childbirth in 1874 was very different to the planned and programmed delivery of modern times. There was no assumption of a happy outcome for either mother or child. Women often died during labour and of all the babies born, around one in six did not live to celebrate their first birthday.

There were no choices to be made as to where and with what method of pain relief the child would be brought into the world. Almost invariably babies were born at home. Natural childbirth was inevitable and a whiff of chloroform the only respite from labour pains, which for twentieth-century women have become an optional extra.

Once born there would have been no incubator for this premature baby. There would be no thought of bonding mother to child, a subject unheard of in those days, and no discussion on the rival merits of breast or bottle. Almost all babies were breast-fed although the provision of a wet nurse for the "privileged few" ensured they did not spoil their mother's figures or interfere with their social life.

A second letter, giving her version of Winston's birth, went the same day from the Duchess of Marlborough to Mrs Jerome.

30 November   *Blenheim*

My dear Mrs Jerome,
    Randolph's Telegram will already have informed you of dear Jennie's safe confinement & of the birth of her Boy. I am most thankful to confirm the good news & to assure you of her satisfactory Progress. So far indeed she could not be doing better. She was in some degree of Pain Saturday night & all Sunday & towards evg of that day we began to see that all the remedies for warding off the Event were useless. Abt 6 of P.M. the Pains began in earnest.
    We failed in getting an accoucheur from Oxford so she only had the Woodstock Doctor; we telegraphed to London but of course on Sunday ev there were no trains.
    Dr Hope only arrived at 9 of this Morg to find dear Jennie comfortably settled in bed & the baby washed and dressed! She could not have been more skilfully treated though had

he been here than she was by our little local doctor. She had a somewhat tedious but perfectly safe & satisfactory Time. She is very thankful to have it over & indeed nothing could be more prosperous.
    We had neither cradle nor baby linen nor any thing ready but fortunately every thing went well & all difficulties were overcome. Lady Camden, Lady Blandford & I were with her by turns & I really think she could not have had more care. She has had an anxious Time and dear Randolph and I are much thankful it is over. I will be sure to see you receive a Bulletin every day.
    We expect today a 1st Rate Nurse. Best love to Clara & Believe me,

                    Yrs sincerely
                    F. MARLBOROUGH

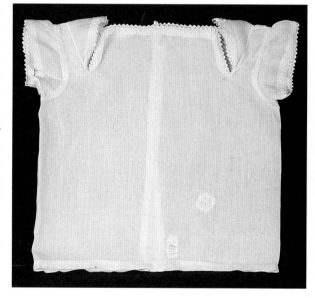

Above: Winston's baby vest
Opposite top: The downstairs room where Winston was born
Opposite: Lord Randolph's letter to Dr. Taylor

Winston was born into a family already firmly written into the history books.

Through his father Lord Randolph Spencer-Churchill, the third son of the seventh Duke of Marlborough, he was descended from John Churchill, Queen Anne's victorious Captain General on whom she conferred the dukedom in 1702. Three years later this honour was followed by the gift of Woodstock Park where, at the Queen's direction, Sir John Vanbrugh built Blenheim Palace.

As the first duke had no surviving sons, an Act of Parliament enabled his title to pass through the female line. Therefore, following the death of his daughter Henrietta, the dukedom passed to the son of his younger daughter Anne and her husband, Charles Spencer. It is from this marriage that the family name of Spencer originated and the Earls Spencer, ancestors of the present Princess of Wales, are descended.

The name of Churchill was retrieved in 1817 from which time all descendants of the Dukes of Marlborough again bore the name of their illustrious ancestor.

Top right: John Churchill, 1st Duke of Marlborough
Right: Sarah, Duchess of Marlboroough
Opposite top left: Henrietta, 2nd Duchess. Top right:
Charles Spencer, 3rd Duke. Middle left: George Spencer,
4th Duke. Middle right: George Spencer-Churchill, 5th
Duke. Bottom left: George Spencer-Churchill, 6th Duke.
Bottom right: John Spencer-Churchill, 7th Duke

Clara Hall   *Leonard Jerome*

While the first Duke of Marlborough was building Blenheim, the first pioneering Jerome set sail for America from the Isle of Wight. Timothy Jerome settled in Connecticut in 1710, his son Samuel moved to Massachusetts and his grandson Aaron, who married Betsy Ball, a cousin of George Washington, farmed in the Berkshire Hills. In 1816 Aaron's eldest son moved his family to Syracuse where Winston's grandfather, Leonard Jerome, grew up.

It was from here that he went to Princeton and, when that proved too expensive, to Union College, Schenectady. Leonard's elder brother, who had paid for his education, then introduced him into the newspaper business.

He married Clara Hall who was to bring new blood into the family. Her grandmother was an Iroquois Indian.

Jennie Jerome was born in Brooklyn on 9th January 1854. Until she was thirteen the Jerome family lived in New York where Leonard Jerome developed his publishing business, eventually owning twenty-five per cent of the *New York Times*. Apart from his dedication to his business affairs, in which he made and lost more than one fortune, Jerome was a man with a variety of interests – yachting, the opera and racing – all of which he pursued in his expansive style. He founded the American Jockey Club in 1866 and the Jerome Park Racecourse which bore his name.

Mrs Jerome had been captivated by European society while her husband had been the American Consul in Trieste from 1851 to 1853. In 1867 Mrs Jerome persuaded her husband to allow her to move with their three daughters to Paris. Here she enjoyed a sparkling social life while the girls were being broadly educated, intellectually, culturally and socially.

They remained in Europe and in August 1873, while staying in the Isle of Wight, the Jerome ladies were invited to a ball on board HMS *Ariadne* at Cowes, to meet the Prince and Princess of Wales. At this ball Jennie was introduced to Lord Randolph Churchill. He was twenty-four. She was nineteen. Three days later they were engaged to be married.

Lord Randolph had a conventional upper-class up-bringing. He was educated at Eton and Oxford after which he travelled extensively in Europe.

The Duke of Marlborough was at first apprehensive at his younger son's precipitate engagement to an unknown American. However, he was mollified when, in deference to his long-held wish, Lord Randolph agreed to stand as the Member of Parliament for Woodstock. The election over, the Duke travelled to Paris in early 1874 where he met and was immediately captivated by his future daughter-in-law.

All opposition thus removed, Lord Randolph Churchill and Miss Jennie Jerome were married at the British Embassy in Paris on 15th April that year.

Above left: Lord Randolph's first letter to Jennie Jerome sent from the Marine Hotel, Cowes
Above right: Lord Randolph
Above: The invitation to the ball with the addition by Jennie

Winston was dressed for the first week of his life in the clothes borrowed from the local solicitor's wife, whose baby was due at the end of January. After a week the borrowed garments were replaced by a more elaborate layette sent by Mrs Jerome from Paris which Lord Randolph reported . . . *has given great satisfaction.* However, the proud father derived less satisfaction from the lack of response from his father-in-law, Leonard Jerome, to whom he had telegraphed the happy news. Despite this silence, Lord and Lady Randolph invited him to be their son's godfather; and, in accordance with the family tradition that the second name should be that of the godparent, Winston was given the second name of Leonard when he was baptised on 27th December in the chapel at Blenheim.

In the New Year the Churchills returned to their house in Charles Street where Winston was cared for by his nurse, Mrs Everest. Lady Randolph's choice of nanny for her son was probably the most important single decision that she made throughout his childhood. Woomany, as he called Mrs Everest, was to become the symbol of home to Winston, the rock upon which he could depend and a strong influence for the next twenty years. Lady Randolph employed a woman who possessed characteristics in complete contrast to her own. Perhaps it was in this difference that lay the success of her choice. In his mother Winston had all the glamour, excitement and unpredictability that anyone could ever want. In Mrs Everest he had a comfortable bosom to cry on, unconditional love and the security of dependability.

. . . **My nurse was my confidante. Mrs Everest it was who looked after me and tended all my wants. It was to her I poured out all my many troubles . . .**

Meanwhile his parents immersed themselves in London society and, as Winston later observed . . . **continued their gay life on a somewhat more generous scale than their income warranted. Fortified by an excellent French cook they entertained with discrimination. The Prince of Wales, who had from the beginning shown them much kindness, dined sometimes with them . . .**

In January 1877, when he was just two years old, Winston travelled to Ireland with his parents and grandparents. His grandfather, the Duke of Marlborough, had been appointed Viceroy, and Lord Randolph

Opposite: Lady Randolph
Top right: Baby Winston
Right: Mrs Everest

accompanied him as his private secretary. The Duke had refused this post several times but on this occasion was persuaded by Disraeli to accept in order that Lord Randolph could withdraw from London society and avoid humiliation at the hands of the Prince of Wales, with whom he had quarrelled and with whom there was even talk of a duel.

The difficulty had arisen when Lord Blandford, the Duke's heir, had become involved with Lady Aylesford, whose husband was a close friend of the Prince. The aggrieved husband threatened divorce. Lord Randolph was aware that the lady had also been the subject of the Prince's attentions and, when he saw his brother being made the scapegoat, spoke of involving the Prince in any divorce action. He was reported as saying "he held the Crown of England in his pocket". In the face of this barely disguised blackmail, the Prince declared that the Randolph Churchills should be ostracised by London society.

Above: Lord and Lady Randolph
Opposite: Winston in his petticoats

Lord Randolph had been true to the Churchill family motto: *Fiel pero desdichado*, Faithful but unfortunate. Winston accompanied his parents into exile.

Winston's development during his time in Ireland is reflected in extracts from letters Lady Randolph wrote to her husband when he returned to London from time to time to attend Parliament.

. . . Winston is flourishing tho' rather X the last 2 days more teeth I think. Everest has been bothering me about some clothes for him saying that it was quite a disgrace how few things he has & how shabby at that . . .

. . . Winston has just been with me – such a darling he is – "I can't have my Mama go – & if she does I will run after the train & jump in" he said to me. I have told Everest to take him out for a drive tomorrow if it is fine – as it is better the stables shd have a little work . . .

. . . I bought Winston an elephant this afternoon which he has been asking me for some time, & I was on the point of saying to the shop-woman "An ephelant" I just stopped myself in time . . .

. . . Winston is flourishing and has learnt a new song "We will all go hunting today etc" . . .

Winston had arrived in Dublin a month after his second birthday dressed, as was the fashion, like a girl. At that time children were dressed alike, making boys and girls indistinguishable one from the other, for the first few years of their lives. This custom continued until the period of post-war austerity following the First World War. Winston's frilly petticoats were gradually replaced by more boyish attire but his vibrant auburn curls were not cut until he was in his fifth year.

It was from Dublin that Lady Randolph wrote the letter to her husband which bears Winston's first smudgy mark.

Irish nationalism had given birth to the Fenians whose aim was to establish an Irish Republic, by force if necessary. . . . My nurse, Mrs Everest, was nervous about the Fenians. I gathered these were wicked people and there was no end to what they would do if they had their way. On one occasion when I was out riding on my donkey, we thought we saw a long dark procession of Fenians approaching. I am sure now it must have been the Rifle Brigade out for a route march. But we were all very much alarmed, particularly the donkey, who expressed his anxiety by kicking. I was thrown off and had concussion of the brain. This was my first introduction to Irish politics! . . .

The fall from the donkey was the first of a series of childhood accidents which were to punctuate Winston's early years.

Mrs Everest was a woman with high principles, strong prejudices and a superstitious nature. Winston spent his first eight years almost entirely in her company and was exposed to all three. As his intellect matured he developed his own opinions but he remained superstitious all his life.

Winston's earliest memories of his mother are of their time in Dublin . . . My picture of her in Ireland is in a riding habit, fitting like a skin and often beautifully spotted with mud.

. . . My mother seemed to me like a fairy princess: a radiant being possessed of limitless riches and power. She shone for me like the Evening Star. I loved her dearly – but at a distance. . .

His feelings can, perhaps, be explained by his mother's undoubted beauty and exceptional personality reflected in the words of Lord D'Abernon, an ambassador and international figure and clearly a fascinated admirer . . . *The Viceroy was on the dais . . . but eyes were not turned on him or his consort, but on a dark, lithe figure, standing somewhat apart and appearing to be of another texture to those around her, radiant, translucent, intense . . . More of the panther than the woman in her look, but with a cultivated intelligence unknown to the jungle.*

While the Marlboroughs lived at Vice-Regal Lodge, the Churchills were in a smaller house close by. It was here that Winston discovered a less agreeable side to life. This is how he remembered it half a century later

Opposite: Lady Randolph with Winston in Ireland

... It was at The Little Lodge I was first menaced with Education. The approach of a sinister figure described as "the Governess" was announced. . . . Mrs Everest produced a book called *Reading without tears* . . . I was made aware that before the Governess arrived I must be able to read without tears. We toiled each day. . . . I thought it all very tiresome. . . . Our preparations were by no means completed when the fateful hour struck. . . . I did what many oppressed people have done in similar circumstances: I took to the woods. I hid in the extensive shrubberies – forests they seemed – which surrounded The Little Lodge. Hours passed before

Above: Lady Randolph . . . in a riding habit, fitting like a skin and often beautifully spotted with mud.
Right: . . . My mother seemed to me like a fairy princess . . . she shone like the Evening Star. I loved her dearly – but at a distance

I was retrieved and handed over to the Governess. We continued to toil every day, not only at letters but at words, and at what was much worse, figures. Letters after all had only got to be known, and when they stood together in a certain way one recognised their formation and that it meant a certain sound or word which one uttered when pressed sufficiently. But the figures were tied into all sorts of tangles and did things to one another which it was extremely difficult to forecast with complete accuracy. . . . The Governess apparently attached enormous importance to the answer being exact. If it was not right it was wrong. . . . These complications cast a steadily gathering gloom over my daily life. They took one away from all the interesting things one wanted to do in the nursery or in the garden. . . . They became a general worry and preoccupation. . . .

My mother took no part in these impositions, but she gave me to understand that she approved of them and she sided with the Governess almost always. . . .

On one occasion an unhappy Winston rang for the maid and when she appeared said, "Take away Miss Hutchinson. She is very cross." By strange coincidence Miss Hutchinson was later governess to Clement Attlee, Deputy Prime Minister in Winston's Coalition Government and his successor when a Labour government was returned to power in the closing days of the war. He reported the governess's description of Winston as "a very determined little boy".

Lord and Lady Randolph's second son, Jack, was born in Dublin on 4th February 1880. Like Winston he was born prematurely, a blue baby given little chance of survival. His condition was so grave that he was immediately christened in the private chapel. Happily for Winston, hitherto a rather lonely only child, and for his parents, whose last child this would be, Jack survived to grow up to be a loyal and much-loved brother and son.

Soon after Jack's birth the Churchills returned to England in order that Lord Randolph could once more fight a general election. Although he personally retained Woodstock for the Tories, the party as a whole was defeated and Gladstone returned as Prime Minister. As a result the Duke of Marlborough's time as Viceroy came to an end. Lord and Lady Randolph moved into St James's Place. They were gradually welcomed back into the circles from which they had been excluded three years before although yet three more years were to pass before there was a complete reconciliation with the Prince of Wales.

Winston in Dublin aged 5

Meanwhile Lord Randolph became increasingly absorbed in politics and began to gain considerable stature in the Tory Party. Simultaneously Lady Randolph threw herself once more into the whirl of London Society. In this situation Winston's needs were subordinated to those of his parents.

Even by Victorian upper-class standards he saw little of them. Still only five, he found himself consigned to the care of Mrs Everest and a peripatetic existence in which the splendours of Blenheim contrasted with more prosaic surroundings on the Isle of Wight.

However, for Winston and Jack there were benefits to be gained from being farmed out for their parents' convenience. The two boys spent several happy holidays on the Isle of Wight. Mrs Everest took them to Ventnor to stay with her sister and brother-in-law, John Balaam, who was a senior warder at Parkhurst Prison. Balaam made a profound impression on Winston. While they walked together over the Downs he regaled the boy with vivid tales of prison mutinies and shipwrecks. The older man found in his young companion an eager participant in discussions about the Zulu War, graphic and bloodthirsty newspaper accounts of which had captured Winston's imagination.

It was probably from Ventnor, in the summer of 1881 when he was six years old, that Winston wrote his first known letter to his mother.

My dear mama I am so glad you are coming to see us I had such a nice bathe in the sea to day. love to papa your loving winston

Opposite: Lady Randolph with Winston and Jack   *Above: the first of many uniforms*

As a result of primogeniture the great estates of England have been kept largely intact. Satisfactory though this system of eldest son takes all may be to the heir, it is of little comfort to his siblings. Lord Randolph, brought up in ducal splendour, once married was to be constantly preoccupied with his lack of money. Convention among the aristocracy precluded sons from salaried employment except in the armed forces or the Church. Lord Randolph had opted for politics and, since Members of Parliament were unpaid, was forced for income to rely on an allowance from the Duke of Marlborough. His family, although welcome at Blenheim, had no country house of their own. Thus Winston and Jack spent a great deal of time under the disciplinarian eye of their grandmother the Duchess.

It would have been extraordinary if the young Winston had not been significantly influenced by the deeds of his illustrious ancestor whose military victories were so magnificently portrayed in the tapestries lining the walls of the State Apartments. It was from Blenheim that Winston wrote to his mother on 4th January 1882.

Above: Tapestries at Blenheim *by Winston S. Churchill c. 1928*

My dear Mamma I hope you are quite well I thank you very very much for the beautiful presents those Soldiers and Flags and Castle they are so nice it was so kind of you and dear Papa I send you my love and a great many kisses Your loving Winston

Monday
My dear mamma I am quite well and getting on very nicely with my lessons Baby is quite well. I am enjoying myself very much. with love and kisses your affectionate W. S. Churchill

Dearest mamma I do want you come down so much. we are going out now. your loving Winston

Life at Blenheim must have been beyond a young boy's dreams. Once Winston's lessons with the governess were over, the possibilities for his entertainment were limitless. There was riding in the park or the riding school, fishing in the lake or putting on a play with his cousins. There were also the treasured visits from his mother when they went for walks together and she read him stories.

Lady Randolph's diary gives an insight into the way she filled her days. A talented horsewoman, musician and painter, she always had something to interest her.

Tuesday January 17th 1882

Cold & Raw. Gave Winston his lessons then painted till luncheon went to the stables – then walked with R – & the Duchess till 5 – read to the children . . . played billiards with the Duke & Ld Alfred Churchill –

Friday February 24th

. . . took Winston & had tea with Blanche H at her lodgings . . .

Twenty-six years after she had entertained the eight-year-old to tea Lady Blanche Hozier became his mother-in-law. Winston married Clementine Hozier in 1908 and . . . lived happily ever afterwards.

Lord Randolph, who had arrived in Dublin a political lightweight, returned to London a serious politician. His time in Ireland and the famine which had struck in his last year there had opened his eyes to human problems and a degree of poverty which he had not previously encountered. It was from this experience that his short but brilliant political career developed. The seven-year-old Winston could not have been unaffected by the stimulating and intriguing atmosphere of his parents' life, both political and social. However, the busier they were the more time he and Jack spent at Blenheim.

Above: Lady Randolph's diary
Top right: Programme for a play put on by Winston at Blenheim
Right: Lord Randolph

March 20th

My dear Papa

I hope you
are getting better.
I am enjoying my
self very much

I find a lot of
primroses every
day. I bought a
basket to put them
in. I saw three
little Indian child-

-ren on Saturday,
who came to see
the house. Best
love to you &
dear mamma.

I am, Yr loving son
Winston

Dearest Mama

It was such
a lovely day
yesterday that
we went for
a drive. I am

sends you
his love I have
been playing
out of doors
at making
encampments
which is great

enjoying my
self here very
much it is so
nice being in
the country
The gardens
and the park

fun. I pretend
I pretend to
pitch a tent
and make
the umbrella
do for it

are so much
nicer to walk
in than the
Green Park or
Hyde Park.
Baby is very
well and

With best love
to you and
Papa
Ever your
loving son
Winston

march 28

My dear Papa I was so delighted to get your letter and thank you very much for it. I do les-sons every morning with Grandmama she is going to London to day and says she will see you to-morrow so I wish I was with her that I might give you a kiss. Please give Mama my love I will write to her soon. And with many kisses to you Your loving son Winston

Left: Winston in another uniform

Blenheim was always to hold a special place in Winston's heart. It was at Blenheim that he was born. It was at Blenheim that he became engaged to be married. It was to Blenheim that he came in the 1930s, when in the political wilderness, to paint the scenes of his childhood and to research the biography of his hero and ancestor John, Duke of Marlborough. And finally it was Bladon churchyard, within sight of Blenheim, that he chose for his last resting place.

Overleaf: Blenheim . . . The gardens and the park are so much nicer than Green Park and Hyde Park

Dearest Papa
I am so glad you are better Baby and I went Thursday and gathered a lot of wild hyacinthes. When we were out on Friday near the cascade we saw a snake crawling about in the grass. I wanted to kill it but Everest would not let me With best love and kisses to you and mama Ever your loving son
Winston

Winston had already met education in the form of a governess but that was a benign experience compared with what was now being planned for him . . . a much worse peril began to threaten. I was to go to school. I was now seven years old, and was what grown-up people in their off-hand way called a "troublesome boy". It appeared that I was to go away from home for many weeks at a stretch in order to do lessons under masters. The term had already begun, but still I should have to stay seven weeks before I could come home for Christmas. Although much that I had heard about school had made a distinctly disagreeable impression on my mind, an impression, I may add, throughly borne out by the actual experience, I was also excited and agitated by this great change in my life. I thought in spite of the lessons, it would be fun living with so many other boys, and that we should make friends together and have great adventures . . . Anyhow I was perfectly helpless. Irresistible tides drew me swiftly forward. I was no more consulted about leaving home than I had been about coming into the world . . .

. . . The fateful day arrived. My mother took me to the station in a hansom cab. She gave me three half-crowns, which I dropped on the floor of the cab, and we had to scramble about in the straw to find them. We only just caught the train. If we had missed it, it would have been the end of the world. However, we didn't, and the world went on.

The school my parents had selected for my education was one of the most fashionable and expensive in the country . . . We had tea with the Headmaster, with whom my mother conversed in the most easy manner. I was preoccupied with the fear of spilling my cup and so making "a bad start". I was also miserable at the idea of being left alone among all these strangers in this great, fierce, formidable place. After all I was only seven, and I had been so happy in my nursery with all my toys. I had such wonderful toys: a real steam engine, a magic lantern, and a collection of soldiers already nearly a thousand strong. Now it was to be all lessons . . .

. . . When the last sound of my mother's departing wheels had died away, the Headmaster

Below: St George's School, Ascot

St. George's Ascot   A Class Room.

St. George's Ascot   Dining Hall.

invited me to hand over any money I had in my possession. I produced my three half-crowns, which were duly entered in a book . . .

Four weeks after his arrival at St George's, Winston celebrated his eighth birthday. With hindsight one can only assume that the happiness and satisfaction expressed in his letters were for the benefit of whoever inspected these before posting. It seems most unlikely that a headmaster as apparently sadistic as the Revd H. W. Sneyd-Kynnersley would have allowed any correspondence to leave his school before he had personally checked it. Of all the letters which survive there is not one that gives any inkling of the cruel treatment meted out to the boys in this establishment.

Corporal punishment was a normal part of school life and Victorian parents did not spend their time worrying about their children's education. Winston's American mother, who always had misgivings about St George's School, went along with her husband's views. Lord and Lady Randolph, having selected the most fashionable and expensive school for their son, would have got on with their life and left Winston to get on with his.

Winston was destined to clash many times with authority during the two unhappy years he spent at Ascot. The first of these encounters was with the Latin master. Given his uninspiring introduction to the classics it would have been surprising if he had warmed to the subject. He never did. One can imagine Winston, nearly fifty years later, grinning mischievously as he recorded for posterity his childhood memory of his first Latin lesson.

. . . Behold me then on a gloomy evening, with an aching heart, seated in front of the First Declension

Mensa	a table
Mensa	O table
Mensam	a table
Mensae	of a table
Mensae	to, or for a table
Mensa	by, with or from a table

What on earth did it mean? Where was the sense in it? It seemed absolute rigmarole to me. However

St Georges school

My dear Papa

I am very happy at school. You will be very plesed to hear I spent a very happy birthday. Mrs Kynersley gave me a little cricket. I am going to send a Gazette wich I wish you to read. With love and kisses I remain your loving son Winston

there was one thing I could always do: I could learn by heart. And I thereupon proceeded, as far as my private sorrows would allow, to memorise the acrostic-looking task which had been set me . . .

In due course the Master returned.

"Have you learnt it?" he asked.

"I think I can say it, sir," I replied; and I gabbled it off.

He seemed so satisfied with this that I was emboldened to ask a question.

"What does it mean, sir?"

"It means what it says. Mensa, a table. Mensa is a noun of the First Declension. There are five declensions. You have learnt the singular of the First Declension."

"But," I repeated, "what does it mean?"

"Mensa means a table," he answered.

"Then why does mensa also mean O table," I enquired, "and what does O table mean?"

"Mensa, O table is the vocative case," he replied.

"But why O table?" I persisted in genuine curiosity.

"O table, – you would use in addressing a table, in invoking a table." And seeing he was not carrying me with him, "You would use it in speaking to a table."

"But I never do," I blurted out in honest amazement.

"If you are impertinent, you will be punished, and punished, let me tell you, very severely," was his conclusive rejoinder.

Such was my first introduction to the classics from which, I have been told, many of our cleverest men have derived so much solace and profit . . .

At the end of Winston's first term Lady Randolph was disappointed both with the school and Winston's performance there. On 26th December she wrote, enclosing the school report, to Lord Randolph who was in Monte Carlo.

. . . I send you the enclosed which is all Kynnersley has sent me as regards Winston. He also sends the bill £55 for next term – to be paid in advance. I must own I think it is rather a strong order to have to pay £52 for one month. As to Winston's improvement I am sorry to say I see none. Perhaps there has not been time enough. He can read very well, but that is all, and the first two days he came home he was terribly slangy and loud. Altogether I am disappointed. But Everest was told down there that next term they meant to be more strict with him. He teases the baby more than ever – when I get well I shall take him in hand. It appears he is afraid of me. I am going to make him write to your mother today . . .

st georges school

My dear Momma

I hope you are quite well. I am very happy at school. You will be very glad to hear I spent on the 9th Decer. a very happy birthday. I must now thank you for your love-ley present you sent me. Do not forget to come down a very happy birthday. With love and kisses Ire=main your loving son.

Winston

Spencer- Churchill.

S. GEORGE'S SCHOOL,
ASCOT.

Report from **Nov. 3rd** to **Dec. 9th 1882.**

Division Master's Classical Report.	Place in **4**th Division of **11** Boys for ½ Term. **11**th	
	Composition	⟍
	Translation	⟍
	Grammar	Has made a start. —
	Diligence	He will do well, but must treat his work in general, more seriously next Term.
Set Master's Report.	Place in **3**rd Set of **14** Boys for ½ Term **14**th	
	Mathematics	Very Elementary. —
	French	Knows a few sentences, but Knowledge of Grammar is very slight. —
	Scripture History Geography.	} fair.
	Writing and Spelling	Writing good but so slow. — Spelling weak. *H. Martin Cooke.*
	General Conduct	Very truthful, but a regular 'pickle' in many ways at present — has not fallen into school ways yet — but this could hardly be expected

Total Place for term 11th.

Times late 4

H. Lockwood Kynnersley
Head Master.

Winston enjoyed riding and, as in other activities which held his interest, he did well. He was soon off the leading rein and immediately wrote to his mother, proudly informing her of his progress.

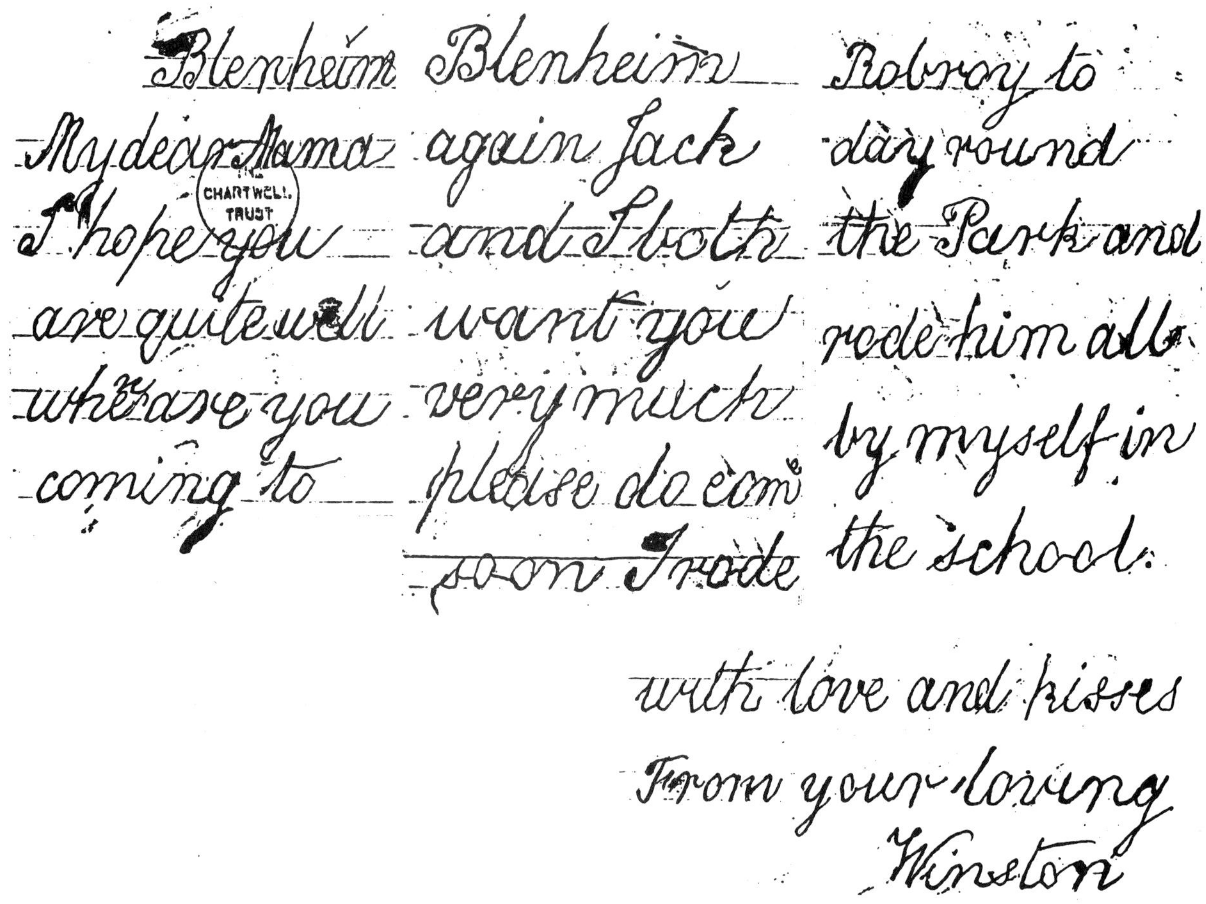

> Blenheim
> My dear Mama
> I hope you
> are quite well
> where are you
> coming to
>
> Blenheim
> again Jack
> and I both
> want you
> very much
> please do com
> soon I rode
>
> Robroy to
> day round
> the Park and
> rode him all
> by myself in
> the school.
>
> with love and kisses
> From your loving
> Winston

Winston's letters frequently contained an impassioned plea for a visit from his parents. These requests were usually in vain but his aunts and other relations did take pity on him.

The faithful Mrs Everest was a regular and welcome visitor. A note, written when she was about to visit him, was left unsigned in his excitement.

Feb 24th 1884

My dear Mamma

I hope you are quite well. I am wondering when you are coming to see me? I hope you are coming to see me soon, dear. How is Jack. You must send somebody to see me. I went out to dinner last sunday with the Alfred Churchills.

with love & kisses
Winston

My dear oom
t I shall see you on
the 31st of this month.

Good-bye

kisses

W. J. J. H.

love & kisses

J

Remain

yours

my dear mamma

I hope you will • come and see me soon. Did Everest give you my flour I sent you. Give my love to my aunts and tell not to forget to come down.

I am comeinge home

In a month.

• loveing

Son

W. L. S. Churchill

XXX

Opposite: The Great Hall at Blenheim *by Winston S. Churchill c. 1928*

It is hard to imagine that such a plea, following hot on the heels of the "flour", could have been denied.

During the summer holidays Winston and Jack had been left at Blenheim. Lord Randolph, who was travelling on the Continent, was concerned who would keep Winston in order. On 9th September he wrote to Lady Randolph from Lucerne . . . *I hope you had a nice time at Blenheim & that Winston was good. I think it is rather rash of you letting him be at Blenheim without you. I don't know who will look after him & Sunny & keep them in order . . .*

Once more Winston wrote to his mother proudly announcing a new achievement. How he would have loved to show off his first fish!

Above: The Lake at Blenheim *by Winston S. Churchill c. 1928*

Sept 15th. 1883.

my dear mamma

I hope you are quite well. I went out fishing to day + I caught my first fish by my-self. Jack + I are quite well. With love + kisses.

I am your loving

Winston

It was not just her hectic social life or lack of interest in her children that kept Lady Randolph's visits to Blenheim as brief as possible. Although by no means maternal she loved her children and enjoyed being with them and no doubt if Lord Randolph had been able to afford a country house of his own things would have been different. His wife did not like being beholden to other people, particularly those with whom she was not in sympathy, as is clearly illustrated in an early letter to her mother.

I quite forget what it is like to be with people who love me. I do so long sometimes to have someone to whom I could go and talk to . . . The fact is I loathe living here. It is not on account of its dullness, that I don't mind, but it is gall and wormwood to me to accept anything or to be living on anyone I hate. It is no use disguising it, the Duchess hates me simply for what I am – perhaps a little prettier and more attractive than her daughters. Everything I do or say or wear is found fault with. We are always studiously polite to each other, but it is rather like a volcano, ready to burst out at any moment . . .

Lady Randolph was being modest, she was an acclaimed beauty and there was clearly jealousy on the part of the Churchill women.

Below left: The 7th Duchess of Marlborough
Below right: The 7th Duke of Marlborough

Winston's letters were those of a very loving son and although he was constantly begging for a visit he gave no indication of his unhappiness at school. However, there is no doubt that he spent a miserable time at St George's. His reports continued to be unsatisfactory but were probably toned down in order not to draw attention to the lack of success the school was making with the son of their most influential parent. The headmaster even found Winston's appetite worth mentioning . . . *He is rather greedy at meals.*

Food was one subject that Winston left unmentioned when recalling his unhappy experiences there . . . **How I hated this school and what a life of anxiety I lived there for more than two years. I made very little progress at my lessons, and none at all at games. I counted the days and hours to the end of every term, when I should return home from this hateful servitude and range my soldiers in line of battle on the nursery floor . . .**

S. George's School,
Ascot.

My dear Mamma.

I hope you are quite well. I had a nice letter from Jack, but I think Everest held his hand. I will try to be a good boy. Anty Leonie has

been staying here at Ascot. I want you to come here for the concert on the 14th of dec Anby is coming to see the concert. With Love and kisses I remain your affect son.

Winston

good by

Winston on his own admission made very little progress. Nevertheless he made a considerable mark. One boy who followed Winston at St George's was Maurice Baring who related . . . *Dreadful legends were told about Winston Churchill, who had been taken away from the school. His naughtiness appeared to have surpassed anything. He had been flogged for taking sugar from the pantry, and so far from being penitent, he had taken the Headmaster's sacred straw hat from where it hung over the door and kicked it to pieces. His sojourn at the school had been one long feud with authority. . . .*

Meanwhile Winston was writing of winning prizes!

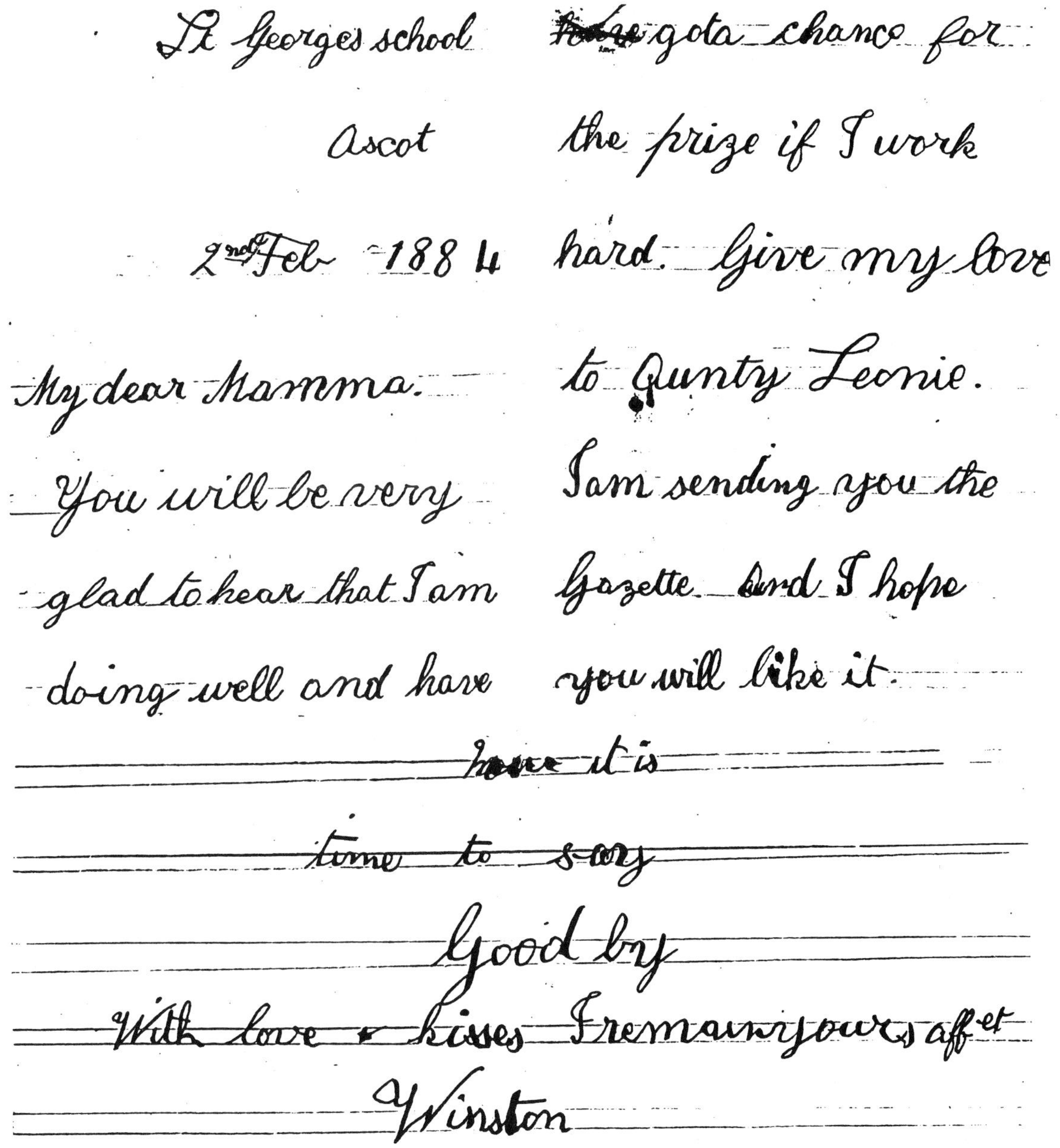

St Georges school

Ascot

2nd Feb 1884

My dear Mamma —

You will be very glad to hear that I am doing well and have

~~have got a chance for~~

the prize if I work hard. Give my love to Aunty Leonie.

I am sending you the Gazette. And I hope you will like it.

~~have it is~~

~~time to say~~

Good by

With love & kisses I remain your affet

Winston

Feb 17th 1884

My dear Papa

I hope you are quite well. It was so kind of you to send me that nice book. I am very happy indeed.

With love and kisses I remain your loving

there was a very wise old man + he was wounded once more

... The greatest pleasure I had in those days was reading. When I was nine and a half my father gave me *Treasure Island*, and I remember the delight with which I devoured it . . .

Winston's feud with authority is unsurprising given his temperament and the brutal nature of the school regime . . . Flogging with the birch in accordance with the Eton fashion was a great feature in its curriculum. But I am sure no Eton boy, and certainly no Harrow boy of my day, ever received such a cruel flogging as this Head-Master was accustomed to inflict upon the little boys who were in his care and power. They exceeded in severity anything that would be tolerated in any of the Reformatories under the Home Office . . . Two or three times a month the whole school was marshalled in the Library, and one or more delinquents were hauled off to an adjoining apartment by the two head boys, and there flogged until they bled freely, while the rest sat quaking, listening to their screams. This form of correction was strongly reinforced by frequent religious services of a somewhat High Church character in the chapel. Mrs Everest was very much against the Pope. She was herself Low Church, and her dislike of ornaments and ritual, and generally her extremely unfavourable opinion of the Supreme Pontiff, had prejudiced me strongly against that personage and all religious practices supposed to be associated with him. I therefore did not derive much comfort from the spiritual side of my education at this juncture. On the other hand, I experienced the fullest applications of the secular arm . . .

Roger Fry, who preceded Winston at the school, gave the following description of Monday morning at St George's where as head boy he was obliged ex officio to assist Mr Sneyd-Kynnersley in his cruel form of correction . . . *In the middle of the room was a large box draped*

St George's school Ascot
Mar 9th 1884

My dear momma
I hope you are quite well. We had Lots of on wednesday. And we all went by train to Bagshot & walked back. now you must tell me about the polls. Has he been chasing any boars lately 30 days more and the Holidays will be

Here

With love and kisses I remain your loving son.
Winston

in black cloth and in austere tones the culprit was told to take down his trousers and kneel before the block over which I and the other head boy held him down. The swishing was given with the master's full strength and it took only two or three strokes for drops of blood to form everywhere and it continued for 15 or 20 strokes when the wretched boy's bottom was a mass of blood . . . he had an intense sadistic pleasure in these floggings.

Harry Graf Kessler, a German boy who was at the top of the school when Winston arrived, recorded his impression of the new boy . . . *Winston Churchill, a grandson of the Duke of Marlborough, at that time a red-haired and restless boy, rather small for his age, who through his exhibitionism and quarrelsome attitude got on everyone's nerves. . .*

He observed that, as a result of the time he had spent in the stables at Blenheim, Winston had . . . *learned words and manners which were highly unsuitable for a young gentleman. Mr Kynnersley reacted with shock and apprehension against the not unlikely possibility that the entire school might adopt the spicy expressions and the readily imitable attitudes of stable lads. When Winston, who was quite tiny – he was only just eight years old – leapt around on a classroom table and recited to an attentive group of boys a little song from the stables, Mr Kynnersley threatened the use of the birch.*

Kessler's description of the school explains why St George's was so popular . . . *Mr Kynnersley ran the school as a preparatory school for the national educational establishments, Eton, Harrow and Westminster, in which* the sons of the ruling caste were educated to become members of parliament, ministers, ambassadors, senior civil servants, high church dignitaries and the leaders of big business, and before long the rulers of the British Empire.

Of the forty boys between the ages of eight and fourteen, ten to fifteen came from the old established landed gentry, a further third from the rich middle class and the remainder from well known families of the English and Scottish aristocracy. . .

Winston's, Roger Fry's and Harry Graf Kessler's accounts, all written many years later, agree on the disciplinarian attitude of the headmaster. Fry, who spent five years at St George's and ended his time there as head boy, came to the conclusion that Kynnersley was stupid rather than sadistic.

Kessler's verdict was . . . *despite the beatings and the very strict regime in the school, Mr Kynnersley was in fact the only real positive influence on him during his schooldays.*

Lord Randolph was now galvanizing the Tory Party which had still to shake off the effects of its electoral defeat four years earlier. His scorn for William Gladstone, the Prime Minister, and condemnation of the government's policies towards working men, earned him a considerable following in the country. When he agreed to contest Central Birmingham, a Liberal stronghold, he became the focal point of Tory democracy, the darling of the party and a household name.

Winston mistakenly dated his letter 1883. It should have read 1884.

1884

Winston was by now, in so far as he was capable, an avid follower of the publicity surrounding his father's political career, the course of which was to have a profound effect upon Winston's own political thinking.

Winston's extravagance had begun to show. Two shillings and sixpence was a princely sum in 1884, being the equivalent of £8 in 1994. He was forever short of money and his letters from this time frequently sought more funds. This was the start of a life-long trend of living beyond his means.

In this letter Winston displays his constant interest in Lord Randolph's political fortunes. His reference to his father concerned Lord Randolph's election to the Committee of the National Union of Conservative Associations. Challenging the traditional leaders of the Conservative Party and their protégés, Lord Randolph had resigned the chairmanship of the Committee but was overwhelmingly re-elected, thereby greatly increasing his influence.

Throughout his childhood Winston's health was a preoccupation both for him and his parents. His premature birth undoubtedly contributed to his less than robust constitution. It was to Mrs Everest he turned for sympathy.

S. GEORGE'S SCHOOL,
ASCOT.

Report from _May 8th_ to _June 20th 1884._

Place in School Order in Division at the end of last Term.	3rd	Present place for ½ Term	3rd

Place in	4th Division of 9 Boys for ½ Term.	
Composition	Wants more care.	
Translation	very fair.	
Grammar	Good.	
Diligence	Better on the whole but still far from satisfactory.	
No. of times late	2. a great improvement.	

Place in	4th Set of 8 Boys for ½ Term		3rd
Mathematics	ought to be better – Careless. —		
French	Good		
German	—		

Scripture	f.
History	} very good.
Geography	
Writing and Spelling	Spelling improved. Writing full of corrections & untidy. —
Music	good.
Drawing	fair. H. Martin Cooke.

General Conduct	better – but still troublesome.
Headmaster's Remarks	He has no ambition – if he were really to exert himself he might get to 1st at the end of the Term.

Head Master.

Herbert W. Sneyd-Kynnersley

By the summer of 1884 it was clear that Winston and St George's were not compatible . . . My teachers saw me at once backward and precocious, reading books beyond my years and yet at the bottom of the Form. They were offended. They had large resources of compulsion at their disposal, but I was stubborn. Where my reason, imagination or interest were not engaged, I would not or I could not learn. In all the twelve years I was at school no one ever succeeded in making me write a Latin verse or learn any Greek except the alphabet. I do not at all excuse myself for this foolish neglect of opportunities procured at so much expense by my parents and brought so forcibly to my attention by my Preceptors. Perhaps if I had been introduced to the ancients through their history and customs, instead of through their grammar and syntax, I might have had a better record.

I fell into a low state of health . . . and finally after a serious illness my parents took me away.

Another version of the way he saw his removal from St George's was given many years later while reminiscing to a young relative . . . If my mother hadn't listened to Mrs Everest and taken me away I would have broken down completely. Can you imagine a child being *broken down*? I can never forget that school. It was *horrible*.

According to contemporary accounts and in keeping with his character, Winston was as badly behaved as any boy in the school. It is therefore certain that he received his share of beatings and, judging by the descriptions of these disciplinary sessions, likely that they would have left their mark. It is possible that evidence of the cruel punishment was spotted by Mrs Everest who informed Winston's mother. Lady Randolph, although no doubt resigned to the ways of her adopted country, would have been outraged. Being an American she was unaccustomed to and had never been quite convinced of the benefits of the barbaric custom, unique to the British upper classes, of sending small boys away to school, let alone sanctioning sadistic schoolmasters to inflict corporal punishment on the children in their charge.

For whatever reason, possibly the harsh discipline but certainly because of his frail constitution, it was decided that Winston should have a change of environment.

After the unhappy start to Winston's formal education, Lord and Lady Randolph decided to adopt a completely different approach in the selection of their son's new school.

Where St George's was fashionable and pretentious, with the headmaster's coat of arms displayed over the front door, the establishment they chose in Brighton was so lacking in pretension that it did not even have a name, just an address, 29–30 Brunswick Road, Hove. In contrast to the sadistic and disciplinarian Sneyd-Kynnersley, the new school was run by two kind unmarried ladies, Kate and Charlotte Thomson.

There is no doubt that, apart from the healthy sea air, the reason for this unusual choice of school was the fact that Dr Robson Roose, the Churchills' family doctor, had his main practice in Brighton and he was therefore able to keep a close watch on Winston whose health was giving cause for concern. Indeed, had his parents chosen a more spartan environment further removed from the attentions of their own doctor, it is unlikely that Winston would have survived the near-fatal illness which was to strike him down eighteen months after his arrival at Brunswick Road.

Winston's recollection of his time at Brighton was much happier than his memories of St George's . . . **there was an element of kindness and of sympathy which I had found completely lacking in my first experiences . . . At this school I was allowed to learn things which interested me: French, History, lots of Poetry by heart, and above all Riding and Swimming. The impression of those years makes a pleasant picture in my mind, in strong contrast to my earlier schoolday memories . . .**

Winston's first term at Brighton, although marred by ill-health, went smoothly enough. He wrote to Lady Randolph about his interest in stamps probably to justify his request for more money.

29 Brunswick R^d
Brighton.
Oct 28th 1884

My dear Mamma,
    I hope you are quite well. I am quite happy here, I have been very extravagant, I have bought a lovely stamp=book. and stamps will you. please send a little more money. Good=bye dear mumy. With Love And kisses, I remain your lov= ing Son
        Winston

X X X V V

To Mrs Everest he complained that he had not been well and that his mother had not written to him.

my dear oom

I have not been very well this week I woke up one morning with a crupy cough Mrs Ottway kept me in bed all days and the next days she would not let me go out but I am all right now. over You must excuse this scribble, as I wrote it in a hurry

I shall soon be looking for a visit from you so you must ask mamma to let you come and see me with Jack. Give my love to him and tell him he may have my little artillery. now I must say good-bye as I am going to give mamma a lecture for not writing to me.

With love and kisses I remain yours affect

Winston

kisses for you
× × × + + + + + + + + + × × × × × × ×
× + × × × × × × × × × × × × × ×

Ps I got 215 marks my frist week and my 2nd I got 285:

While Winston was settling into his new school, his father's political career was gaining pace. His position in the Conservative Party and his popularity in the country could no longer be ignored. As a result of an informal agreement with Lord Salisbury, the Tory leader, Lord Randolph set off on a tour of India in December. This was to serve two purposes, to restore his failing health on the long sea voyages and to acquaint him with India and its problems, in preparation for his entry into the next Conservative government as Secretary of State for India.

Lady Randolph took Winston and Jack to see him off. Winston returned to Brighton for the last two weeks of term. He wrote to his father.

Dec. 5th, 1884
Brighton

My dear Papa
I hope you had a good passage and were not sick at all on board?
Was it rough at all?
I should like to be you on that beautiful ship. We went and had some Turtel soup after you went, so we did not do amiss. We saw your big ship steaming out of harbour as we were in the train. I cannot think of anything more to say. With love and kisses I remain yours affect
Winston
P.S. I had not any foriegn Paper, so you must excuse me.

Lady Randolph was concerned that she might not be able to control Winston during the Christmas holidays. Mrs Everest, loved and confided in by her charges, was by now indispensable to her employer who wrote to Lord Randolph . . . *The children have both gone – I shall have Jack back before Xmas as I cld not undertake to manage Winston without Everest – I am afraid even she can't do it . . .*

Above: Lord Randolph
Opposite: Winston and Jack

Dec 5ᵗʰ 1884

Brighton

My dear Papa
I hope you had a good passage and were not sick at all on board?.
Was it rough at all?

I should like to be you on that beautiful ship We went and had some Turtel soup

At home or at school Winston was obviously a handful. Just before the Christmas holidays he was involved in a scrape which caused Miss Thomson to write to Lady Randolph.

29 Brunswick Road
Dec. 17th

Dear Lady Randolph Churchill

Soon after writing to you this morning, I was called to see Winston who was in a trouble that might have proved very serious. He was at work in a drawing examination, and some dispute seems to have arisen between him, and the boy sitting next to him about a knife the tutor had lent them for their work. The whole affair passed in a moment, but Winston received a blow inflicting a slight wound in his chest.

Dr Roose assures me that he is not much hurt, but that he might have been. As this was not the first time we have had to complain of a very passionate temper in this boy, I decided to send him home at once. He is a candidate for the Britannia [a naval training establishment], and if it is known that he is expelled, he will be disqualified. I have told his parents that if you wish him to be publicly expelled, I shall do it; but I leave that decision to you. If you approve the milder course he will quietly disappear from the school, and we shall think the punishment sufficient. I am quite sure that it is very necessary to impress upon these young boys the necessity of their learning to govern their passionate impulses, and so serious a punishment falling on one of their school fellows, will I hope, help to do so.

Dr Roose tells me that Winston is going to town with him on Friday; so he will be able to give you his medical report.

Believe me
very faithfully yours
Charlotte Thomson

Lady Randolph, under no illusion as to Winston's part in the incident, insisted that the boy should not be expelled. She wrote the same day to her husband *. . . Jack came back from Bournemouth yesterday looking most fit. Winston arrives with Dr Roose today – I was much startled yesterday by receiving the enclosed from Miss Thomson – I had a telegram from Dr Roose at the same time saying that Winston was all right – but fancy what a serious affair it might have been! – I have no doubt Winston teased the boy dreadfully – & it ought to be a lesson to him – I will not close my letter until I have seen him & can tell you how he is – His holidays are not over until the 20th of Jan. I hope I shall be able to manage him – I mean to make him do a little writing etc every morning . . . Dr Roose and Winston have just arrived – the latter is all right – the penknife however went in about a quarter of an inch but of course as I thought he began by pulling the other boy's ear – I hope it will be a lesson to him . . .*

Lord Randolph received his wife's letter on his arrival in Bombay. Judging by the tone of his reply sent on 9th January, he apparently took the news of Winston's latest misdemeanour very lightly.

My dearest

I have just telegraphed to you wishing you very many happy returns of the day, & now reiterate the same with every wish that you were out here with me. I got your long letter of the 19th on Tuesday on arrival here from Beejapore; What adventures Winston does have; it is a great mercy he was no worse injured . . .

His only other reference to Winston's adventure is in a letter written from Lucknow on the 24th January *. . . Also tell little Winny how glad I was to get his letter which I thought was very well written. I suppose he is back at Brighton now. I hope there will be no more stabbing . . .*

Jan 21ˢᵗ 1885
29 Brunswick
Road

My dear Mamma
        I hope you are well.
I am getting on pretty
well. The Play is on
the 11ᵗʰ of February 1885.
You must be happy
Without me, no sereems
from Jack or complaint.
It must be heaven upon
earth. Will you try and
find out for me what day
Dr Rouse is going to take
me to see Dr Woaks write
and tell me. Will you
tell me what day the
mail goes to India, because
I want to write to him.

This letter, written to Lady Randolph following his return to school after the Christmas holidays, shows that Winston had a clear understanding of the difficulties his mother had controlling him.

The reference to his appointment with Dr Woakes, a Harley Street aural surgeon and the author of a book *On Deafness, Giddiness and Noises in the Head*, is the first indication that it was acknowledged that Winston had a problem with his ears and therefore probably his balance. This, combined with a speech defect, was a challenge he had to overcome throughout his life and was undoubtedly the reason that so many seemingly minor childhood scrapes became full-scale incidents.

Now I must say
good-bye.
With Love and kisses
I remain
        Your Loving son
        Winston

29 & 30, BRUNSWICK ROAD,
BRIGHTON.

The Misses Thomson,

desire to announce that the ensuing Vacation

will commence

Thursday April 2ⁿᵈ

The School will re-open

Tuesday 21ˢᵗ April

and the Misses Thomson request the

punctual attendance of their pupils.

N.B.—Pupils travel under escort by the following trains:—
Leaving Brighton at 9.45 a.m., arrive at Victoria at 11.7 a.m.
Leaving Victoria at 1.30 p.m., arrive at Brighton 5.45 p.m.

Winston's introduction to chemistry was altogether a happier experience than his first encounter with the classics.

24-30 Brunswick Rd

Brighton Jan 28th

My dear Mamma.

I hope you are quite well. I have rider three times a week, I have one hour on Tuesday, an hour and a half on Wednesday, and an hour on Friday. Do you think Papa will stay long in India?. Have you heard from him lately?. Is Jacky quite well and happy? does he cry at all now? I am quite well and, very happy. How is old Chloe, has she been shaved yet?. I make my pony canter when I go out riding. I will send you a list of the work we have. A master here is going to give a lect-ure on Chemistry, is it not wonderful to think that water is made of two gases nam-ely Hydroydgen and ~~Nitrogen~~. I like it, only it seems so funny that two gases should make water. With love and kisses.

I remain,

Your loving son

Winston

29 + 30 Brunswick

April 8th 1885

My darling Papa,

I hope you are quite well. The weather continues very fine though there has been a little rain lately I have been out riding with a gentleman who thinks that Gladstone is a brute and thinks that "the one with the curly moustache ought to be Premier" The driver of the Electric Railway said "that Lord R Churchill would be Prime Minister" Cricket has become the foremost thought now. Every body wants your autograph but I can only say I will try, and I should

Although Lady Randolph was apparently resigned to Winston's bad behaviour, she was still preoccupied with his feeble health, as can be seen in her letter of 13th February to Lord Randolph . . . *I went to Brighton to see Winston yesterday – & took Jack with me – They were so happy together & Winny was wildly excited but I thought he looked very pale and delicate, & Miss Thomson said that she thought he was far from strong – What a care the boy is! – He told me he is very happy, & I think he likes the school but I fancy that he does not get out enough – We witnessed a performance of a play in which Winston appeared as a woman "Lady Bertha" & he acted quite wonderfully & looked so pretty – I shall see Roose in a day or 2 & will have a talk about him . . .*

like you to sign your name in full at the end of your letter I only want a scribble as I know that you are very busy in= =deed. With love and kisses
I remain
Your loving son
Winston

Until he went to boarding school Winston lived his life in the protected confines of his family environment. Whether at Blenheim, at home in London or visiting Mrs Everest's prison warder brother-in-law on the Isle of Wight, Winston's only contact with anyone outside his immediate family was with those who worked in the house or on the estate, all of whom would have treated *Master Winston* with the respectful intimacy of old family retainers.

The realisation that his adored and respected but remote father was a figure of national admiration seems to have been brought home to him during his eleventh year. It is unlikely that Winston did not reveal his identity with pride to his riding instructor, or to **the driver of the Electric Railway**, but it was encounters of this kind that made him aware of Lord Randolph's fame.

The other boys at school were also impressed by the celebrity among them and Winston lost no time in turning this to his advantage. By a steady trade in his father's autograph he attempted to satisfy his ever-increasing need for funds.

Randolph S. Churchill

29 + 30 Brunswick Rd
Brighton, Apr 24th

Dearest Papa,
          I got here all right on Tuesday. I hope you are quite well. Will you write and tell me where Mamma is staying, what is her address? The weather is lovely and we have begun Cricket. I am in the 1st Eleven as extra man. I should be very proud if you would write to me Papa. With love and kisses
          I remain
          Your loving
          Son
          Winston

Within a few weeks his first foray into the world of commerce was proving so successful that he decided to branch out and test the value of his mother's autograph as well.

Lenin Randolph Churchill LONDON. DUBLIN.

29 + 30 Brunswick Road
9th May 1885.
Brighton W

My dear Mamma;
I hope you are quite well. Have you recovered your good health again as I expect you were rather frightened when the shaft went into your leg. I am looking for an=other letter from you. I rec'd a nice letter from Papa this morning. he sent me half a dozen autographs I have been busy dis=tributing them to-day every body wanted one, but I should like you to send me a few ot yours too. I must now say Good = bye I remain your. loving son Winston.

29 & 30, BRUNSWICK ROAD.

Lower School.—Class 4th

Report of Winston Leonard Spencer Churchill

Term beginning January 20th — ending April 2nd /85

	Marks gained.	Highest gained.	Position in Class.	No. in Class.	REMARKS.
Scripture Knowledge	495.	730.	5.	8.	Very satisfactory progress made during the Term. C. J.
English Subjects	2864	4093	4.	10.	
Mathematics	647.	1472.	7.	10.	
Classics	1488.	2010.	4.	10.	
French	1270.	1855.	4.	10.	
German					
Music					
Drawing	11.	55.	8.	18.	
Conduct	135.	582.	29.	29.	

School will re-open Tuesday, April 21st /85

Winston, who had been described as greedy by his first headmaster, was, like most small boys, always hungry. He was not impressed by the food at Brunswick Road where he reported he was given only half a sausage for breakfast, undoubtedly an exaggeration by a child accustomed to the plentiful nursery breakfasts at home and perhaps with the wistful picture of the glimpses he had of the grown-ups helping themselves from a sideboard groaning with food laid out in rows of silver dishes.

It took over four months for Lady Randolph to despatch the **long promised hamper** for which Winston had been campaigning since March.

She probably had other things on her mind as it was at this time that Lord Randolph was appointed Secretary of State for India. The Tories had brought down the Liberal government and Lord Salisbury was now Prime Minister.

Above: Lord Salisbury

29 + 30 Brunswick Rd.
T Brighton
June 30th 1885.

Dearest Mamma,
        I am quite well, and hope you are the same. I have been to the dentist to-day. I have rec.d the long promised Hamper. We are going for a picnic on the 17th of July. There are only 28 more days before the end of the term. With love and kisses I remain,
                Your loving son,
                Winston

Tuckers Hotel
Cromer. Aug 20th/85.

Once again Winston and Jack were sent to a seaside hotel in the care of Mrs Everest and a governess.

This was not Winston's most successful holiday. The weather was bad, the unkind governess made him do needlework, he felt ill and bad-tempered and wanted his mother.

My dear Mamma

I have not been enjoying myself bad- = ly, lately : The wea= = ther has been very rainy lately.

I am working a tle Yept for you, in wool. Will a you allow me write once a week instead of twice. I am quite well and happy,

to get out between the showers,

——
—— " ——

Jack sends love.

With love & kisses

I remain

Your loving

Winston

x x + + x x x x x + o x x +

P.S. Please excuse the writing as I have*

* want

Cursed with a fragile constitution, Winston about this time developed an uncommon preoccupation with his health. His dependence on a thermometer became a feature of his adult life during which he took his temperature every day.

Chesterfold Lodge.
Cromer, 2nd Sept.
—

My dear Mama
          I have rec'd your letter this morning. The weather is very fine, But, I am not enjoying myself very

much. The governess is very unkind, so strict and stiff, I can't enjoy myself at-all. I am counting the days. H till Saturday, then I shall be able to tell you all my troubles.

I shall have ten whole days with you. I like the stamps very much indeed. My temper is not of the most amiable but I think it is due to the liver, As I have had a

billious attack which thoroughly upset me, my temperature was 10,0 once instead of 98 of which is normal. With love and kisses I remain Your loving W. Churchill

29 + 30 Brunswick Rd.

Oct 10ᵗʰ 1885.

Mama dear

I have got leave
to write a private letter.
And so you will excuse
writing. I enclose a
Photo of my self.
& ask if you will
be so kind as to
send me the sum
half a quid or 10 bob
if you know what
that is. I want to
get 2 doz. more and
I will send you.
some. Fans flourishing
With love & kisses
I remain.
Your loving son
Winny

P.S. This was taken by a boy who is at this
school

For a child, who had not yet reached his eleventh birthday, to have twenty-four potential recipients of his photograph shows an unusual degree of confidence and self-importance. He had probably seen his father's secretary responding to requests for Lord Randolph's photograph and, basking in the reflected glory, perceived a similar value in his own. In fact Winston did not integrate easily and the only friend he ever mentioned in particular at this time was Bertie Roose, the son of the family doctor. Despite the fact that the other children may have been impressed by Winston's famous father and his grand relations, it would not have made them like him any better. Undoubtedly his bumptious nature and intellectual precocity, combined with an aggressive temperament, made him unpopular with his own age group.

29/63 Brunswick Rd
Brighton
Oct 20th 1885.

Dearest Papa,

I cannot think why you did not come to see me, while you were in Brighton, I was very disappointed but I suppose you were too busy to come.

I have got 708 stamps from foreign parts and I want to get a stump Album, I reckon, guess, and cal-culate that the volumes would come to about 17/6, it may be 17/6½ for all I know but I think I could manage with-out the ½, I hope you will grant my mild request.

The weather is very bracing here. Will you give my love to mam-ma. With love & kisses

I remain

Your loving son
W. Churchill

P.S. Look out for post-scripts

Throughout his schooldays Winston was hardly ever visited by his father and, certainly in his own eyes, insufficiently by his mother. Neglectful though this may seem in the twentieth century, Victorian parents, once they had dispatched their sons to school, did not feel obliged to spend their time going to see them. What a relief it must have been for the lonely Winston to be able to find in the approaching election a valid reason for the lack of attention from his parents, even when his father failed to visit him when in Brighton on political business.

Winston's letters were on the whole supervised and, even under the more relaxed regime of the Thomson sisters, probably censored. From time to time he **got leave to write a private letter**. On these occasions his letters varied from untidy to scribbled, in marked contrast to the beautifully formed handwriting of some others written, no doubt, in official letter-writing sessions. Also his use of English, with which he was starting to experiment, became much more relaxed. It is unlikely that the authorities would have approved the use of the words **quid** or **bob**.

My dear Mamma

I am not very happy. But quite well. I want you to come and see me when the Elections are over. I recᵈ 2/6 many thanks Tell Dom I got my coat.. give my best love to Dom and Jack. I want two more Pencils. With Love I remain. Your loving son Winny

half a quid or 10 bob if you know what that is.

29 + 30 Brunswick Road,
Brighton,
Novem.br 28th 1885.

Dearest Papa,
I hope most sincerely that you will get in for Birmingham, though when you receive this the Election will be over.

There is another whole holiday to-morrow. There is a boy here whose Papa is going to put up for Winchester he is a Conservative, his name is Col. Tottenham. If he gets in for Winchester and you get in for Birmingham I Believe we are going to have a supper..

With much love,
I remain,
Ever your loving son,
Winston Churchill.

Above: Lord Randolph at his desk

In the General Election in November 1885, Lord Randolph, whose Woodstock constituency had disappeared in a redistribution of parliamentary boundaries, stood in the Liberal stronghold of Birmingham. He was defeated but, when an admirer stood down in his favour, was elected the following day for South Paddington.

Colonel Tottenham was also elected, so the supper was able to take place.

Winston was very protective of his young brother and throughout his schooldays very proud of his progress which was much steadier than his own.

February 1886   **Brighton**

Dear Jack,

Thank you so much for your nice letter it was very good – Vous avez fait beaucoup de progrès dans votre écriture.

Quant à le combat en Trafalgar Square voici une petite illustration . . . your writing is much improved – you are now making great progress in every way. Try and make a difference between the up strokes and the down ones as =

Dearest Jack Remember me

Try also to get on in your work.
Because if Mama sees that you are getting on you will not have to go to school next year. When I come home I must try and teach you the rudiments of Latin.

Winston was referring in the fourth line to a meeting of unemployed organised by the "Revolutionary Social Democrats" in Trafalgar Square on 8th February 1886 at the end of which a mob rampaged through the streets.

Winston wrote to his mother on 14th February 1886, concerned for her safety after the riots. He continued his letter on a pleading note asking her to allow Mrs Everest and Jack to stay on in Brighton to be near him. The request was evidently granted as he wrote again on 23rd February telling her . . . I have been out to dinner to-day to see Everest and Jack, and enjoyed myself very much.

Feb. 14th 1886.

My darling Mummy,

I trust you will not be the object of any malice at the hands of the London Mobs. I have a little plan to ask, namely := to let Oom and Jack stay a little longer at Brighton. It makes me feel so happy to think that my Oom an Jack are down here, so you will let them stay here, wont you?.

With much love.

Iremain

Your loving
W. Churchill

going to take place? I have been out to dinner to-day to see Everest and Jack, and enjoyed myself very much. With love & kisses,

Iremain,

Your loving son,
Winston Churchill

My dearest Mum

I rec'd your letter.

Jam feelings very
weak, & I feel as
if I could cry at
every thing.

I was all right,
after you left, till
just this evening

With love & kisses
Jremain

Yours affect

Winston

After his beloved nurse and younger brother had returned home, Winston wrote to Mrs Everest. This was the most pitiful of all his letters.

Thanks to the care given to his patient by Dr Roose, it was not to be his last but with hindsight it can be seen that the letter reflected the fragile condition of the writer.

Within a few days Winston was in bed with pneumonia. For five days he clung to life. Dr Roose barely left his side and his parents rushed to Brighton.

Dr Roose reported continuously to Lord Randolph.

4 Sunday 10.15 p.m.   29 & 30 Brunswick Road
[14 March 1886]   Brighton

Memo: W. Churchill
Temp: 104.3 right lung generally involved – left lung of course feeling its extra work but, as yet, free from disease! Respirations more frequent. Pulse increased!
NB This report may appear grave yet it merely indicates the approach of the crisis which, please God, will result in an improved condition should the left lung remain free.

I am in the next room and shall watch the patient during the night – for I am anxious.

Robson Roose

6 a.m.
[15 March 1886]
. . . The high temp indicating exhaustion I used stimulants, by the mouth and rectum, with the result that at 2.15 a.m. the temp had fallen to 101, and now to 100, thank God. I shall give up my London work and stay by the boy today . . .

1 p.m.
[15 March 1886]
. . . We are still fighting the battle for your boy. . . . As long as I can fight the temp and keep it under 105 I shall not feel anxious . . .

11 p.m.
15 March 1886
. . . Your boy, in my opinion, on his perilous path is holding his own well, right well! The temp is 103.5 at which I am satisfied, as I had anticipated 104! There can now be no cause for anxiety for some hours (12 at least) so please have a good night, as we are armed at all points . . . Pardon this shaky writing. I am a little tired. . . .

16 March 1886
. . . We have had a very anxious night but have managed to hold our own the temp. is now 101, the left lung still uninvolved, the pulse shows still good power and the delirium

I hope may soon cease and natural sleep occur, when one might hope he would awake free from the disease – on the other hand we have to realize that we may have another 24 hours of this critical condition to be combatted with all our vigilant energy. I have telegraphed that I remain here today . . . I have given you a statement of fact, your boy is making a wonderful fight and I so feel please God he will recover.

Letters of sympathy came from friends and colleagues. On 16th March Sir Henry James wrote to Lady Randolph:

Tuesday   *28 Wilton Place*
Belgrave Square

My dear Lady Randolph,
  I do hope you will believe how much sympathy is felt for you & your husband in this anxious time. I most sincerely hope that the prospect is brightening.
                       With love Yours most truly
                       HENRY JAMES

And on the same day Lord Salisbury wrote from Monte Carlo to Lord Randolph . . . *I am very sorry indeed to have just heard that you have had anxiety about one of your sons at Brighton. I earnestly hope it is entirely removed by this time.*

When Robson Roose reported at seven in the morning of 17th March, the end of the crisis was in sight . . . *I have a very good report to make. Winston has had 6 hours quiet sleep. Delirium has now ceased. Temp: 99, P.92, respiration 28. He sends you and her ladyship his love . . . I will call in on my road to the station . . . I shall not return tonight . . . I will however come down tomorrow night or Friday as the lung will I hope begin to be clearing up and must be carefully examined. I leave the case in Rutter's hands in whom I have every confidence.*

His letter to Lady Randolph, written at Brighton station as he was returning to London, indicated there was still cause for concern.

[17 March 1886]   *The Station [Brighton]*

Dear Lady Randolph Churchill,
  Forgive my troubling you with these lines to impress upon you the absolute necessity of quiet and sleep for Winston and that Mrs Everest should not be allowed in the sick room today – even the excitement of pleasure at seeing her might do harm! and I am so fearful of relapse knowing that we are not quite out of the wood yet.
Yrs faithfully and obliged
Robson Roose

Even at Buckingham Palace Winston's health was a subject of conversation. When reporting the Prince's concern, Moreton Frewen, the husband of Lady Randolph's sister Clara, took the opportunity to make an oblique criticism of his sister-in-law's attention to his nephew. He expressed the hope that she would *make more of him* in the future.

17 March 1886   *18 Chapel Street*
Park Lane

My dear Jennie,
  It is such a relief to us all to hear that you regard the crisis as past; I am so glad you dear thing. Poor dear Winny, & I hope it will leave no troublesome after effects, but even if it leaves him delicate for a long time to come you will make the more of him after being given back to you from the very threshold of the unknown.
  Everyone has been so anxious about it; The Prince stopped the whole line at the levée to ask after him, & seemed so glad to hear (on Monday) that he was a little better.
  Bless you both; when do you come back?
                       Yours ever
                       M

Above: The Prince of Wales

It had been a very close call and care had still to be taken. The bonus for Winston was that he did, for a brief period, see more of his father.

On 17th April Winston was convalescing at home in Connaught Place when Lord Randolph wrote to Lady Randolph . . . *Winston is going on well & attended by Dr Gordon. He cannot go out yet as the weather is raw with a NE wind. He is in great delight over a Locomotive steam engine I got for him yesterday . . .*

Winston's recovery was obviously complete when he wrote to his mother eight months after the illness.

23rd November 1886   Brighton

My dear Mama,

I hope you are quite well.

Whatever you do do not forget to write to Miss Thomson, to ask her to allow me to come home on Saturday 27th of the 11th month of 1886.

You may imagine what a treat it will be to me. We had a Gymnastic Examination on Monday, I find that in Addition to having gained back my strength I have gained more than I possessed before, I will give you an Illustration "Last Christmas term I beat Bertie Roose by 1 mark, Last term he beat me by 10 marks. This term I beat him by 3 marks getting top of the school by a majority of 1 mark. I got 60 out of 64.

I am in good health. It is superfluous to add that I am happy.

With much Love, I remain, Your loving son
Winston Churchill

LORD RANDOLPH CHURCHILL,
CHANCELLOR OF THE EXCHEQUER.
1886

After the election in July 1886, Lord Randolph, following his success at the India Office, was appointed Chancellor of the Exchequer and Leader of the House. At the time no one could have imagined that his brilliant political career was shortly to come to an abrupt end. After five months at the Treasury Lord Randolph resigned over his colleagues' refusal to accept a reduction in the military estimates. He was never to hold office again.

29 & 30 Brunswick Rd
Brighton

My darling Mummy,

I hope you are well.

Has Everest gone for her holiday yet? I should like you to come and see me very much. I am very glad Papa got in for South Paddington by so great a majority; I think that was a victory! I hope the Conservatives will get in, do you think they will?

Give my love to Jack and Everest.

With love and kisses
I remain
Your loving son
Winston. S. Churchill

A still frail-looking Winston accompanied his mother to a garden-party in Richmond. Having to sit still surrounded by so many pillars of Victorian England would not have been his idea of entertainment. Riding and chasing butterflies with Jack at Blenheim later on that summer was much more to his taste.

Sept 7th/1886

My dear Mamma

I am enjoy-ing myself very much I have caught a good many Butterflies and Dragon-Fly.

I had a beautiful ride to day. Jack send you a lttle his love and a 6.666666.666666.6666 6.666 kisses. And I

send you double.

With much love
— Tremain
Your loving son
Winston. S. Churchill

Although he was an enthusiastic correspondent, Winston's letters varied considerably in quality. His occasional excursion into a pretentious style was the result of an adverse reaction to a previous letter.

29 & 30 Brunswick Rd.
Brighton
5/10/86

My dear Mama,

I have much joy in writing "Ye sealed Epistle" unto thee. I will begin by informing you the state of the weather, after that, I will touch on various other equally important facts. I received your letter and intend to correspond in the best language which my small vocabulary can muster. The weather is fearfully hot. We went to the Swimming Baths to-day. I nearly swam the length which is about 60 feet in length. We are going to Play a Football Match to-morrow. Last night we had a certain Mr. Beaumont to give a lecture on Shakspeare's play of Julius Caesar. He was an old man, but read magnificently. I am in very good health and am getting on pretty well. Love to all.

I remain,
Your loving son,
Winston. S. Churchill

The fact that his parents were not just well known, but that their attendance was a considerable commercial asset to any venture, could not have helped the already-precocious Winston to develop any modest characteristics.

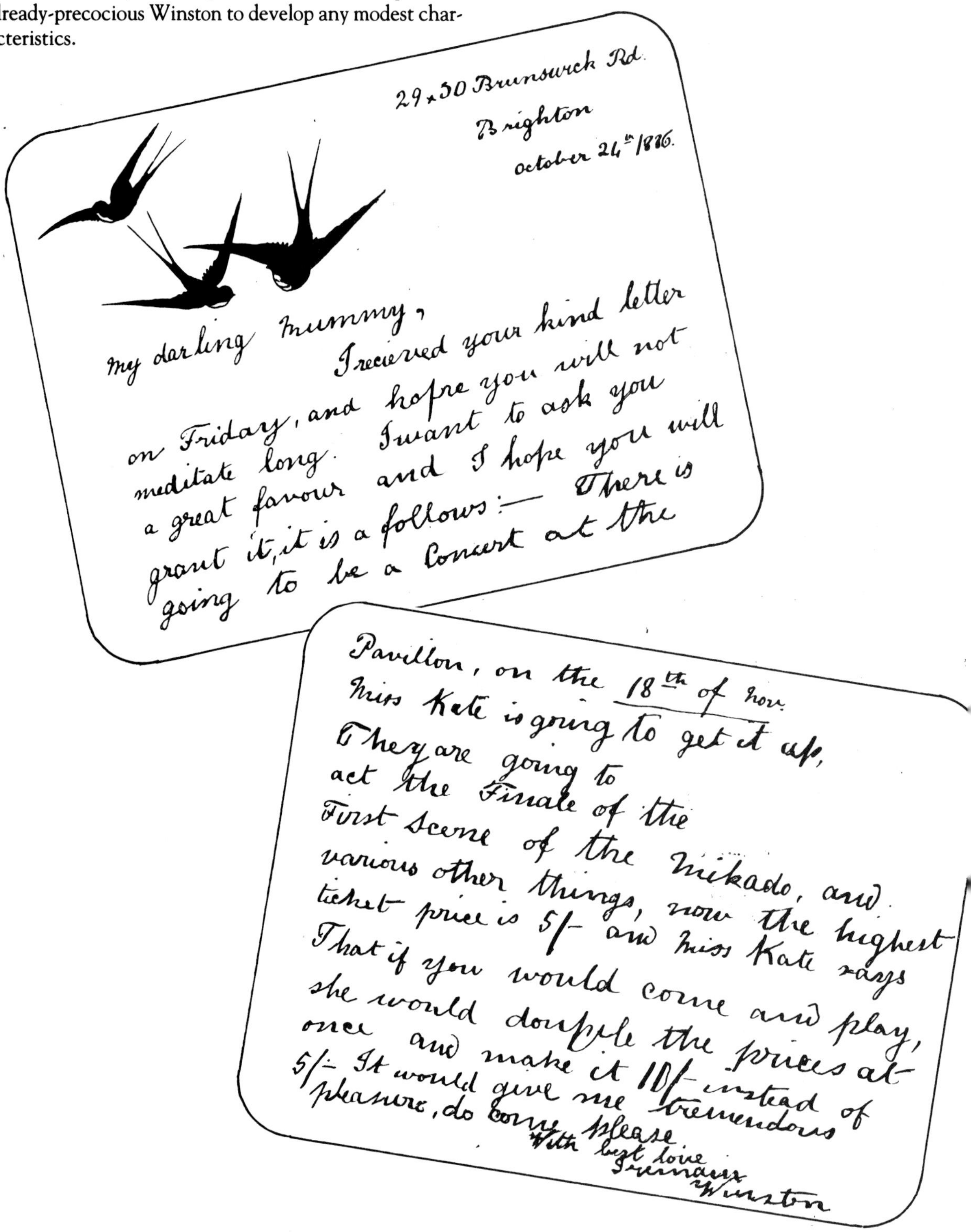

29 & 30 Brunswick Rd.
Brighton
october 24ᵗʰ 1886.

my darling mummy,

I recieved your kind letter on Friday, and hope you will not meditate long. I want to ask you a great favour and I hope you will grant it, it is a follows:— There is going to be a Concert at the Pavillon, on the 18ᵗʰ of nov. Miss Kate is going to get it up, They are going to act the Finale of the First Scene of the mikado, and various other things, now the highest ticket price is 5/- and miss Kate says That if you would come and play, she would double the prices at once and make it 10/- instead of 5/- It would give me tremendous pleasure, do come please.

With best love
Trimaux
Winston

After the unaccustomed attention from his parents as a result of his illness, life for Winston settled down to normal. Which meant that he again began to feel neglected. On 10th November he wrote to his father **... You never came to see me on Sunday when you were in Brighton ...** On 7th December he wrote to Lady Randolph ... **I am working hard at the Play ... Mind and come down to distribute the prizes.** A week later he was still trying to persuade his mother to do as he wanted, suggesting how she should plan her other activities in order to achieve this.

29+30 Brunswick Rd
Brighton
Decem 14.

My darling Mama,
I hope you will not think my command unreasonable or exorbitant, but I nevertheless I shall make it all the same. Now you know, that you can't

2.
be watching a Juvenile Amateur Play in the brother borough of Brighton, and at the same time be conducting a dinner party at
"2 Connaught Place
London.
If you go up to town in time for the dinner party you will not be

3.
able to see the Plays, but simply distribute the prizes and go. Now you know I was always your darling and you & can't find it in your heart to give me a denial, "I want you to put off the dinner party and take rooms in Brighton and go back on

4.
Monday morning,,,, and perhaps take me with you. No II is more moderate, "not bring Jack if inconvenient but come alone, and go back by about the 10-30 PM train, bring Jack if you can. I am quite well and hope you are the same. to be continued.

5.
You know that mice are not caught without cheese." Programme is as near as I can guess as follows — English Play
French play
Latin & Greek
& Recitations.
Supper
Dancing.

6.
commencing 4-30 pm ending 12 pm.
This petition I hope you will grant.
Love to all. I remain
Your loving son
Winston S Churchill.

While the seven-year-old Jack was writing to his mother not only in perfectly formed handwriting but also in French, Winston was signing this untidy letter **The Pussy Cat.** He always liked cats and when, twenty years on, he married Clementine Hozier, his term of affection for her was *The Cat.* His love of animals was returned when, almost eighty years later, as Winston's life ebbed away, his faithful marmalade cat sat on his master's bed and kept vigil until the end.

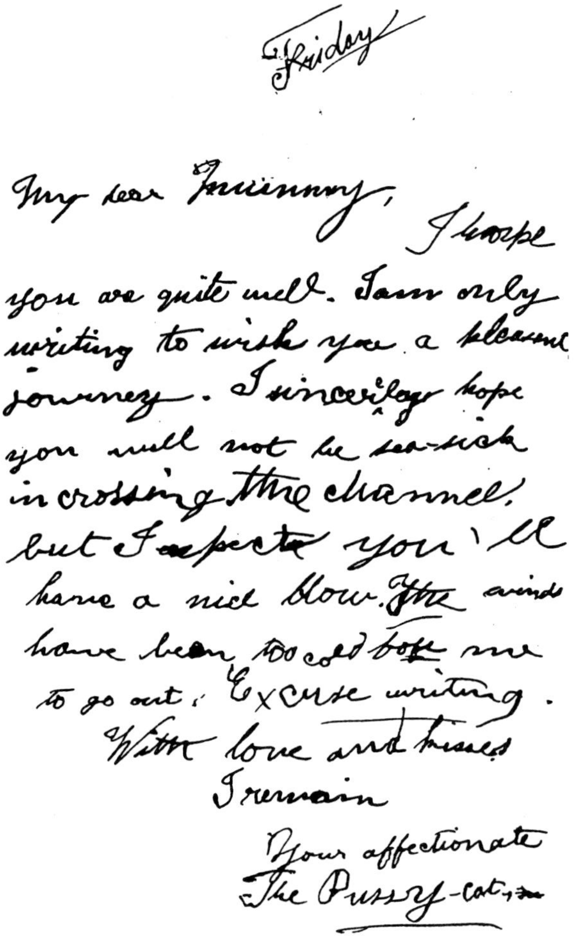

Friday

My dear Mummy,

I hope you are quite well. I am only writing to wish you a pleasant journey. I sincerely hope you will not be sea-sick in crossing the channel, but I expect you'll have a nice blow. The winds have been too cold for me to go out. Excuse writing.

With love and kisses I remain

Your affectionate
The Pussy-cat.

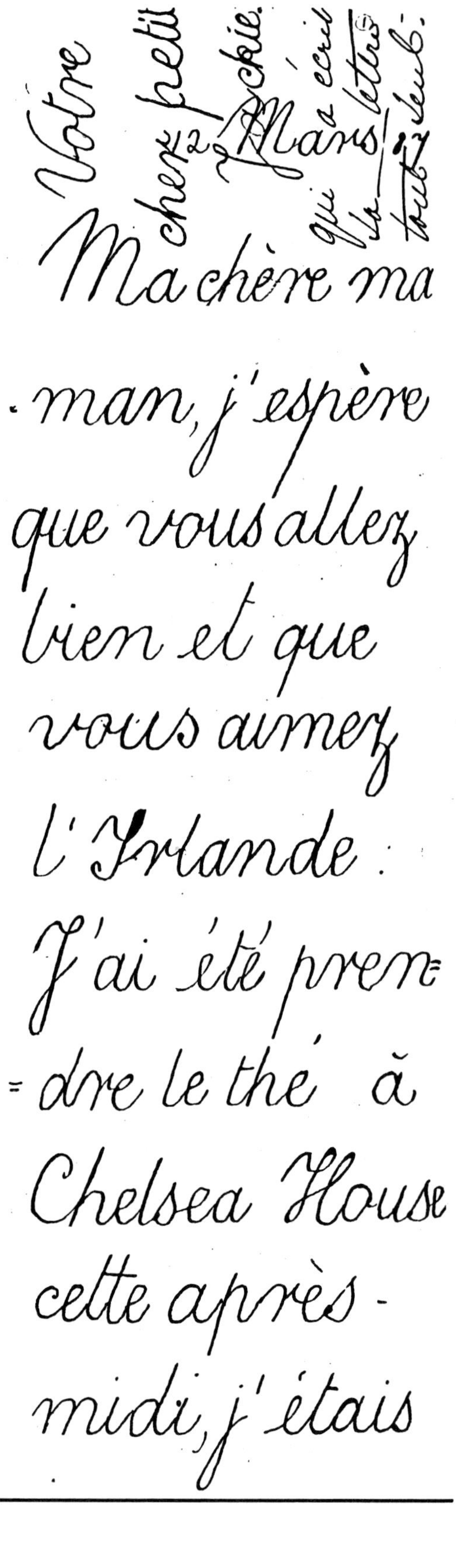

Ma chère maman, j'espère que vous allez bien et que vous aimez l'Irlande. J'ai été prendre le thé à Chelsea House cette après-midi, j'étais

Votre cher petit Jackie.

2 Mars

qui a écrit Un lettres tout seul.

bien content.
Nous avons
joué à beaucoup
de jeux très-
amusants. Ns

avons reçu
une lettre de
Ninny. Un
bon baiser de

Above: Lady Randolph with Jack and Winston

The extremes of mood experienced by Winston are clearly demonstrated in three letters all written to his mother in the same week. He swings from copper-plated cockiness when she has pleased him to utter dejection and scribbled pleading when he feels let down. These periods of depression were a forerunner of **The Black Dog** which was to be a feature of his adult life.

29 & 30 Brunswick Rd.
Brighton
17/5/87.

My dear Mama;

I had the pleasure yesterday morning, of receiving an Epistle from thee, and in return intend to gladden thy heart with one from me. I am quite well. Rather a blunt sentence but you will think it very satisfactory, I have no doubt.

I saw grandmama on Sunday.

I am going out tomorrow with Aunt Wimborne.

Mind & come down on 21st.

Love to All

I remain

Your loving son

Winny

Dear Momma,

It is impossible for you to come on monday it is not a half holiday and so you are going to have a concert and it would not amuse you or I to stay at the school all day. I am chief feature in it. I am very disappointed indeed. but couldn't you come Sunday a stay till Monday I should like it so much I would not mind kicking the Concert off, I have so many things to tell What ever you do Come monday Please. I shall be miserable If you don't.

Love + Kisses

Your loving son

29 + 30 Brunswick Rd.

Brighton

24/5/87.

My dearest Mother,

Will you soon oblige me, by a line or two to let me know if you arrived safely. I did not fill a bit dull after you left yesterday. About a dozen

Diploma, for I want to belong to yours most tremendously. The ices and the bath did not have any effect upon my constitution. I again visited the baths today and got on capitally.

I am, stop! I must not be too egotistical, getting

boys have joined the Primrose League since yesterday, I am among the number + intend to join the one down here, and also the one which you have in London. Would you send me a nice badge as well as a paper of

on well in Cricket and slowly improving. I wish the Jubilee was here avery much. I also hope that you will think my little letter more sensible.

Tremaux

Your loving son

Winny.

The Primrose League, which Winston was intent on joining, and of which he became the Grand Master half a century later, was a grass-roots organisation which provided the Tory Party with voluntary help at elections. At this stage a large part of Winston's interest in political life stemmed from filial loyalty. Three months earlier Lady Randolph had written to her husband . . . *Winston was taken to a pantomime in Brighton where they hissed a sketch of you – he burst into tears – & then turned furiously on a man – who was hissing behind him – & said "Stop that row you snub nosed Radical"!!* Lord Randolph was delighted and rewarded his son's partisanship with a sovereign.

Below: Lady Randolph

29-30 Brunswick Road
Brighton
Sunday

My dear Mamma,
 I hope you are as well
as I am. I am writing this letter
to back up my last. I hope you
will not disappoint me. I can
think of nothing else but Jubilee.
Uncertainty is at all times
perplexing write to me by return
post please!!! I love you so
much dear Mummy and
I know you love me too much
to disappoint me. Do write to
tell me what you intend to
do. I must come home, I felt
I must. Write to Miss Thomson
a letter after this principle
so ÷ "My dear ——
 Could you allow
Winston to come up to London,
on Saturday the 18th for the
Jubilee. I should like him
to see the procession very
much, and I also promised him
that he should come up for the
Jubilee.
 I remain
 Yours
 J. S. C.,,

I think that the above will hit
its mark, anyhow you can
try. I know you will be
successful.
I am looking forward to seeing
Buffalow Bill, yourself, Jack,
Ernest, and home.
I would sooner come home for
the Jubilee and have no amusement
at all than stay down here
and have tremendary fun.
The weather is fine.
Please, as you love me, do as I
have begged you.
 Love to all
 I remain as ever
 Your loving son
 Winny

"For Heaven's sake Remember"!

When he exercised sufficient perseverance, Winston usually managed to get his own way with his mother. He had to muster all his powers of persuasion to convince Lady Randolph to allow him to go to London for Queen Victoria's Golden Jubilee celebrations.

15th June 1887   **Brighton**

Dear Mamma,
    I am nearly mad with suspense. Miss Thomson says that she will let me go if you write to ask for me. For my sake write before it is too late. Write to Miss Thomson by return post please!!!
                    I remain Your loving son
                             Winny

Left: Brunswick Road decorated for the Jubilee
Below: Queen Victoria. A supplement to the Queen *magazine, 1 December 1887*

29-30 Brunswick Rd.
Brighton
24/6/87

My dear Mamma,

I arrived here alright yesterday, and took a cab to the school, at which I arrived at 7½. I am settling down alright now, though rather dull at first. The weather is beautifully fine, we went to the baths to day they were fine. I hope you will ~~soon~~ forget my bad behaviour while at home, and not to make it after my pleasure in my summer Holidays. I telegraphed to Everest as soon as I arrived at the station. All serene. .

Kim came back to day, another boy will come back tomorrow, so I was not the latest back.

I am getting on capitally in Euclid. I and another boy are top of the school in it we have got up to the XXX Proposition. Will you send me a book to read I have got nothing at all to read now. I should like "She" or "Jess" very much indeed — I am quite well.

Please be quick and send me the autographs 6 of yours + 6 of Papa's.

With much love
I remain
as ever
Your loving Son
Winny

W S Churchill

Below: Mrs Jerome with her daughters and grandchildren. Lady Randolph is standing with Winston at her side and Jack in front. Clara Frewen is seated left and Leonie Leslie is seated on the right.

Winston's behaviour while in London for the Jubilee was predictably unsatisfactory. Having tried to make amends with a chatty letter optimistically cataloguing his academic successes, he then made his request for books and more autographs. Judging by his flourishing signature in addition to the often-used **Winny**, he was beginning to experiment with his own autograph.

29 & 30 Brunswick Rd
Brighton
12/7/87

My dear Mamma,

I am looking forward to the Holidays tremendously now! I hope to have very happy ones. Do you think Bertie Roose could come too

It will be double pleasure for me. The weather is nice and fine. Please be quick with the "Autographs" "Book" + "5/-". I should like them at once. I was tremendously surprised by the news I received on Sunday.

We did enjoy our selves tremendo~ at Bramber. Do you think you could come down to see me on Saturday I want to tell you so many things. We went to the Swimming – Baths this morning. I am quite well. With Love + Kisses I remain Your loving Winny

This letter was written more in hope than expectation as the surprising news was that Winston was to have a tutor for the holidays. He acquiesced to this on his own terms . . . I am told that "Mr Pest" is going to be my tutor in the holidays. Now as he is a master here and I like him pretty well I shall not mind him at all, on one condition v.i.z. "Not to do any work" . . .

Left: Winston and Jack with Bertie Roose

Lord Randolph had a brilliant mind, an amazing memory and a gift for languages evinced by his fluency in French and German and his mastery of Latin. Winston did not inherit his father's gift for languages and had yet to demonstrate his own remarkable memory. His attitude to work and authority led Lord Randolph to have no high opinion of his intellectual capacity. However, when he arrived in Cowes to join a rare family holiday, Lord Randolph was surprised at the impression Winston had created with the Prince of Wales who was known, affectionately and irreverently, as Tum-Tum, because of his portly physique. Lord Randolph wrote to his mother on 8th August telling her how the Prince had taken the boys out sailing on the Royal Yacht and that . . . *Tum seems much taken by Winston & told me yesterday I had better retire altogether & Winston was much cleverer than ever I had been.* . . .

The second part of the boys' holidays, spent in a boarding house in Skegness, was in complete contrast to the elegance and grandeur of Cowes and the Royal Yacht. Mrs Everest, in an attempt to curb Winston's extravagance, wrote on the back of his letter to Lady Randolph to justify her refusal to release more money for the coconut shies on the beach. To someone with Mrs Everest's Low Church values such wanton waste would have been deeply shocking.

If Mrs Everest failed to restrain Winston's extravagant spending habits, she was a great deal more influential when it came to matters of religion.

Once their son had been christened, there is no record of any further efforts by Lord and Lady Randolph to influence Winston in the spiritual side of life. Any omission in this area on the part of his parents was, however, more than compensated for by the strong views of his nurse. She continued by virtue of her firm handling, constant presence and, above all, her unconditional love, to be the rock of security to which Winston clung throughout his childhood. It is therefore not surprising that, as feelings of adolescent rebellion stirred within him, it was the anti-Catholic crusade of his beloved Nanny that he espoused. He treasured the proud memory of his stand against authority.

. . . My partiality for Low Church principles which I had acquired from Mrs Everest led me into one embarrassment. We often attended the service in the Chapel Royal at Brighton. Here the school was accommodated in pews which ran North and South. In consequence, when the Apostle's creed was recited, everyone turned to the East. I was sure Mrs Everest would have considered this practice Popish, and I conceived it my duty to testify against it. I therefore stood stolidly to my front. I was con-

Prospect House
Skegness

My dear Mamma,

Forgive me for not writing to you before. I am enjoying myself very much indeed. It was very fine yesterday; but ? to day. I am in good health. I am looking forward to going to Blenheim. May I ask for 2/6.

Love & kisses from

Winny

PS. excuse writing

Master Winston is continually asking for money I give him all the little pleasures that are good for him but he wants to go & knock down cocoa nuts on the sands & wastes a great deal of money. I am nothing else he has applied to you as I do not think it wise to give him money to throw away

CHAPEL ROYAL, NORTH STREET, BRIGHTON.
COPYRIGHT

scious of having created a "sensation". I prepared myself for martyrdom. However, when we got home no comment of any kind was made upon my behaviour. I was almost disappointed, and looked forward to the next occasion for a further demonstration of my faith. But when it came, the school was shown into different pews in the Chapel Royal facing East, and no action was called for from any one of us when the creed was said. I was puzzled to find my true course and duty. It seemed excessive to turn away from the East. Indeed I could not feel that such a step would be justified. I therefore became willy-nilly a passive conformist.

It was thoughtful and ingenious of these old ladies to have treated my scruples so tenderly. The results repaid their care. Never again have I caused or felt trouble on such a point. Not being resisted or ill-treated, I yielded myself complacently to a broad-minded tolerance and orthodoxy.

Winston's mother might easily have been affronted by her letter being enclosed with one that he had written to Mrs Everest. There is, however, no indication that Lady Randolph was ever offended by or jealous of the intimate relationship between Winston and his nanny, or indeed of the influence she had over him. He clearly loved them both but in a very different way. With Mrs Everest he could always be himself; with his mother he sometimes felt the need to make an effort and to show himself in the best light.

Above: The Chapel Royal, Brighton

29 & 30 Brunswick Rd.

Brighton

27/9/87

Dear Mama,

I received your letter yesterday. I read Papa's speech, or rather part of it, on Sunday. My breeches have not turned out badly. I have not begun boxing yet. I am afraid you have forgotten all about "she" please remember, as I am longing to read it.

My Conduct Marks are at present

(10). 10. 10, 8, 9, 7, 10. the best I have ever had.

With love & kisses,

I remain,

Your loving son,

Winston.

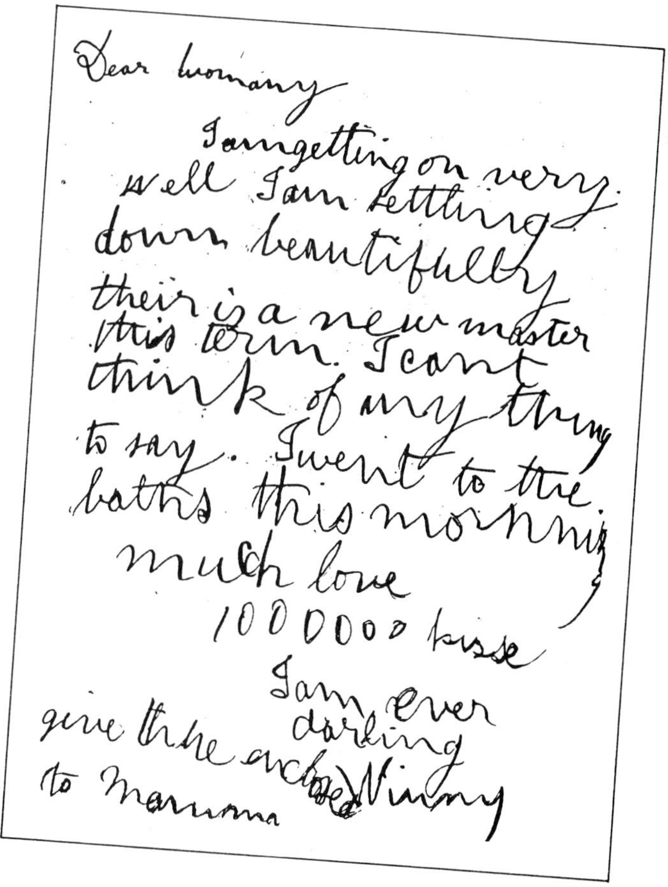

Dear Womany

I am getting on very well I am settling down beautifully their is a new master this term. I cant think of any thing to say. I went to the baths this morning

much love

1000000 kisses

I am ever darling Winny

give these to Marnma

Oct^br 23rd 1887

My dear Papa I hope you are quite well. I am writing to ask you if you will kindly send me two or three of your autograph;s. Also one of your Photograph's for Frances Guest

who is staying here at the Norfolk Hotel. Grandmama Duchess is coming here to-morrow. Miss Thomson says — Winny iss a very good boy and is working in real ernest. He is going to write a Greek play for Christmas. Winny sends you his best love. I have enjoyed my stay in Brighton. with much love from Your loving son Jack Churchill.

The seven-year-old Jack also decided to try his hand at the family autograph business. His very serious letter to Lord Randolph, written while visiting Winston at Brighton, is more like that of an older son commending his younger brother to their father.

The letter mentions visits by their cousin, Frances Guest, and their grandmother the Duchess. Although Winston may have justifiably felt a lack of parental visits, both his and Jack's letters show that there was a steady stream of other relations passing through Brighton.

In December Winston began to plan the Christmas festivities. He wrote to Lady Randolph on the 13th December.

Dearest Mother,
    I have not written to you lately but I will try to write now.
    I am very hard at work what with French Play and Examinations. You said you would not mind a "scribble" if I wrote you 1 decent letter a week.
    When Papa came down he asked Miss Thomson to let us have a half-holiday and she let us have one.
    We will not have a Christmas tree this year, But I think a good 3 guinea Conjuror and a Tea and amusements and games after tea would answer better . . . I must now say good bye
        With love and kisses I remain, Your loving son
            Winston S. Churchill

Winston's letter was written shortly after his father had visited him at Brighton and taken him out for tea. For Winston this was a significant treat. Lord Randolph's request for the boys to be given a half-holiday, a favour traditionally reserved to mark royal visits, indicates the esteem in which he was held. Winston's pleasure was short-lived. The following day he was bitterly disappointed to be told that his parents were leaving for a seven-week visit to Russia.

14 December 1887   Brighton

Dearest Mother,

Miss Thomson told me your plans before your letter arrived. I am very disappointed at hearing that I must spend my holidays without you. But I am trying to make the "Best of a bad job". We shall not be Able to have a party of course. Try and get Mr Best to stay with me and Jack in the holidays. Jack will not want a governess if Mr Best comes. I shall see you on Saturday and I have no doubt you will try your best to make me happy.

           I remain, your loving son
           Winston

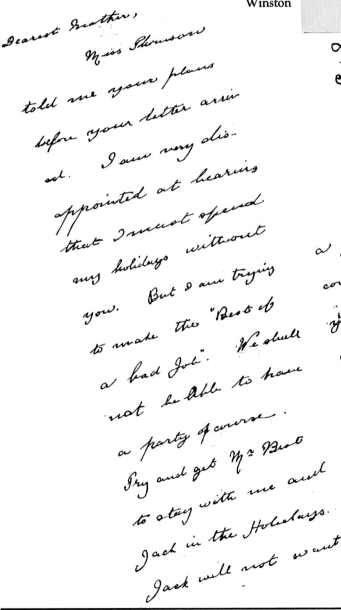

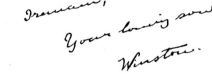

45, HILL STREET,

BERKELEY SQUARE, W.

Winston and Jack were cared for by Mrs Everest until after Christmas when she became ill with diphtheria. They were then looked after by the faithful Dr Roose until the Duchess of Marlborough took them to Blenheim at the New Year. It was a very sad letter that Winston wrote to his mother on 30th December.

Dearest Mother,

I suppose you have heard about Everest's illness. I & Jack at present (Sat. 30) are staying at Dr. Roose's. It is very hard to hear — We feel so destitute.

Dr. Gordon says that Everest has 2 patches down her throat but that it is more Quinsy than Diphtheria.

Darling I hope you will come down to see me, & when you come home and bring Everest

I feel very dull — worse than sad. I must now end Thank you for your letter.

Good bye my dear

I remain

Your loving son

Winston S. Churchill

When he wrote to his mother from Grosvenor Square on 12th January Winston was more cheerful.

Dearest Mother,

Grandmamma had kindly allowed us to sleep here until you come back. I do long to kiss you my darling Mummy. I got your kind letter yesterday. How I wish I was with you in the land of the "Pink, green & blue roofs."

We have been staying at Blenheim lately – it was very nice. Everest is much better – thanks to Dr Roose. My holidays have been chopped about a good deal but as I expect an exeat in the term I do not wish to complain. It might have been so much worse if Woomany had died. You will let me come up for a week to see you & Woomany I am sure.

I am going to a play called "Pinafore" tonight (Thursday) with Olive Leslie.

Tomorrow I am to Dr Goodson's Party. Sat Sir G. Womwell is going to take me to Drury Lane so I am making up for other inconveniences. Auntie Leonie & Auntie Clara gave me together a beautiful theatre which is a source of unparalleled amusement.

I must perform before you when you come back. Have you heard that Uncle Jack has resigned the army? Having told you all the news.

I remain With Love & Kisses, Your loving son
Winston S. Churchill

The Duchess wrote to Lord Randolph that Winston required a firm hand . . . *The boys are very well. The gov is a nice sensible person & seems to be quite happy about them. they leave here & go to Grovr Sq tomorrow so you might write (or Jennie might in your name) a line to B for having them here. It has done them good & I keep Winston in good order as I know you like it. He is a clever Boy & really not naughty but he wants a firm hand. Jack requires no keeping in order. They stay at 46 till you return . . .*

The Duchess was clearly relieved when it was time for Winston to return to school. She wrote to Lord Randolph on 23rd January . . . *Winston is going back to school today. Entre nous I do not feel very sorry for he is certainly a handful. Not that he does anything seriously naughty except to use bad language which is bad for Jack. I am sure Harrow will do wonders for him for I fancy he was too clever & too much the Boss at that Brighton school. He seems quite well & strong and happy – Jack is a good little boy & not a bit of trouble . . .*

Lord Randolph wrote to the Duchess from the British Embassy in Berlin early in 1888 . . . *I always told you Winston was a handfull and you would not believe me. He*

wants a great deal of school. I think it was awfully good of you taking them in. Jack is a real good boy . . .

Winston was clearly growing out of the school at Brighton and in any event it was time for him to move on to public school. It had been arranged for some time that, instead of going to Eton, his father's old school and therefore the obvious choice, he would go to Harrow. The principal reason for this decision was the continuing concern for his health and the benefit to be derived from the bracing air on the Hill.

Winston's letter, written as his parents returned from Russia, was preoccupied both with which house he would enter and the outcome of the entrance examination which he was to sit six weeks later.

7/2/88   Brighton

Dearest Mother,

I received your letter this morning, it was so nice to see it without a Russian Stamp on it. I am longing so, to see you & Papa, it is such a long time since I saw you. I hope it has been arranged which house I am to go to; I want to go to "Crookshank's" as I know a boy there & I should like to be with him. I am working hard – very hard to get in – I only hope that my efforts will be rewarded. Mr Best says that I am certain to pass the Entrance – but he wants me to try & pass the "Farther" as it is called – meaning an Exam which would give me a good place. He wants me to try and get in at the Shell about the middle, he says that I have a pretty fair chance. I have been moved into the VIth Form & have begun "Virgil", which I like and also "Herodotus in Greek".

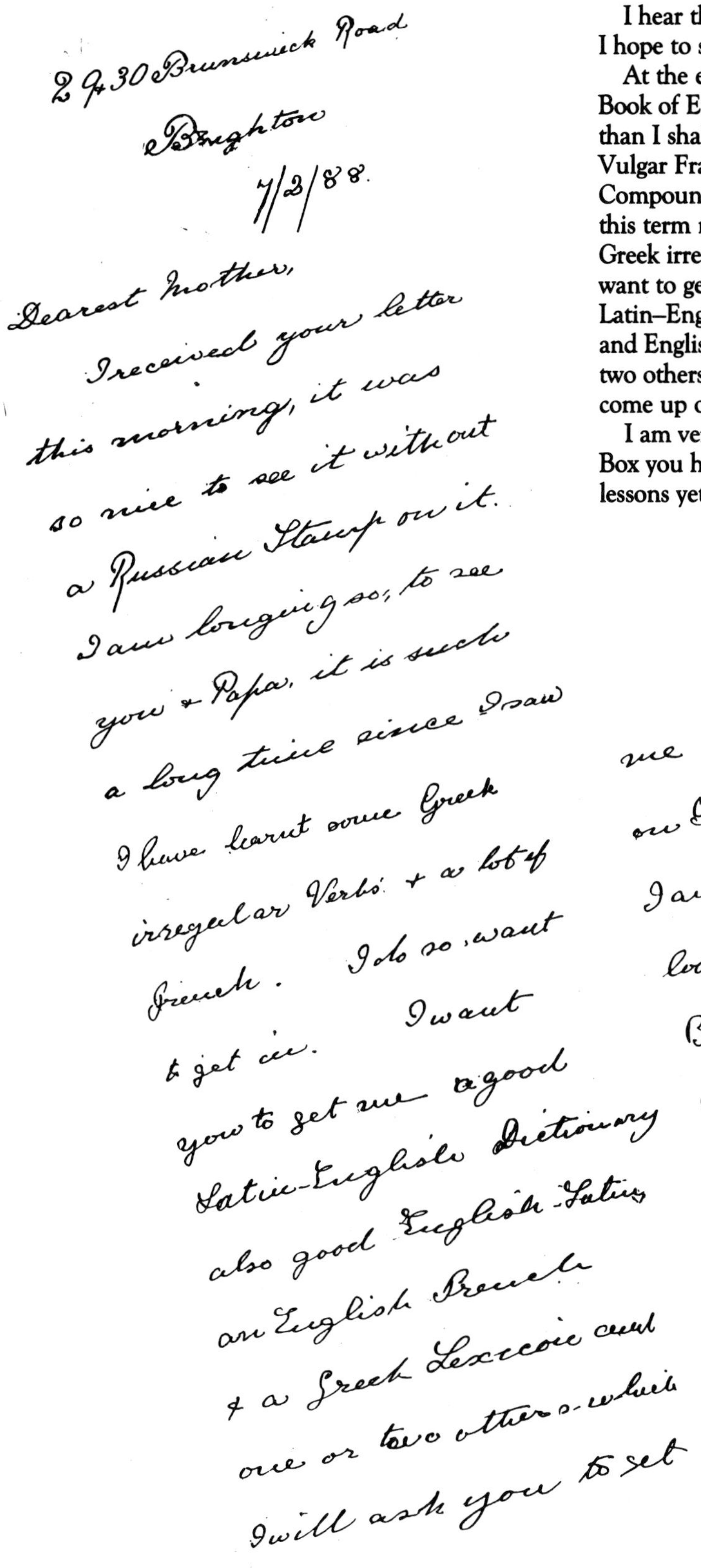

2 & 30 Brunswick Road
Brighton
7/2/88.

Dearest Mother,

I received your letter this morning, it was so nice to see it without a Russian Stamp on it. I am longing so, to see you & Papa, it is such a long time since I saw

I have learnt some Greek irregular Verbs & a lot of French. I do so want to get in. I want you to get me a good Latin–English Dictionary also good English–Latin an English–French & a Greek Lexicon and one or two others – which I will ask you to get

I hear that Algebra is an Extra Subject and so I hope to score in that as I am very fond of it.

At the end of this term I shall know the first Book of Euclid perfectly, which will be more than I shall want. They only require in Arithmetic, Vulgar Fractions, & Decimal Fractions & Simple & Compound Interest, which I know. I have already this term made some progress. I have learnt some Greek irregular Verbs & a lot of French. I do so want to get in. I want you to get me a good Latin–English Dictionary also good English–Latin and English–French & a Greek Lexicon and one or two others – which I will ask you to get me when I come up on Saturday.

I am very anxious to look at the wonderful Box you have bought. I have not begun my boxing lessons yet.

Love to All
I remain, Your loving son,
Winston S. Churchill

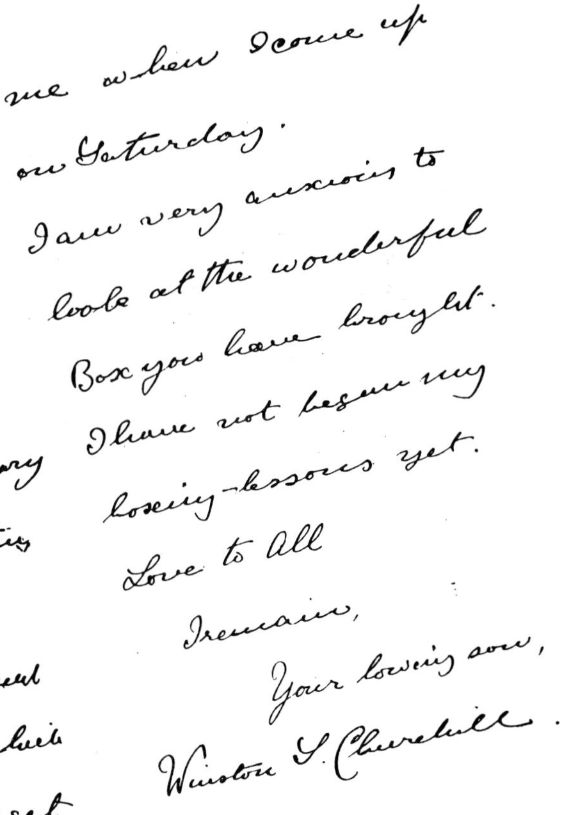

This was the moment in Winston's school life when ... I entered the inhospitable regions of examinations, through which for the next seven years I was destined to journey. These examinations were a great trial to me. The subjects which were dearest to the examiners were almost invariably those I fancied least. I would have liked to have been examined in history, poetry and writing essays. The examiners, on the other hand, were partial to Latin and mathematics . . .

Apprehensive though he undoubtedly was, Winston's account of his preparation for his Entrance Examination for Harrow showed an enthusiastic approach and an optimistic outlook.

6/3/88   Brighton

Dearest Father,

I am working hard for my Examination which is a very Elementary one, so there is all the more reason to be careful & not to miss in the easy things . . . I hope I shall Pass – I think I shall . . .

Will you come down & see me after the Exam & I will tell you all about it.

I will take your advice about doing the most paying questions first & then the others.

Please come down and see me afterwards. Give my love to Mamma.

Miss Thomson has got the Dictionaries but I have not seen them yet. Write to me & let me know if you will come down or not.

Hoping you are well, I remain, Your loving son
Winston S. Churchill

This introduction to examinations was to set a pattern which Winston's later reflections succinctly describe . . . I should have liked to be asked to say what I knew. They always tried to ask what I did not know. When I would have willingly displayed my knowledge, they sought to expose my ignorance. this sort of treatment had only one result: I did not do well at examinations . . .

The visit to Harrow seems to have been almost as much an ordeal for Miss Thomson, who accompanied him, as for Winston himself.

16 March   Brighton

My Lord,

I hear from Mr Welldon today that Winston passed the examination yesterday.

My worst fears were realised with regard to the effect the

nervous excitement would produce on his work: and he has only scraped through.

He was terribly upset after his morning's work and assured me over and over again that he had never translated Latin into English so of course he could not do the piece of prose set on the paper.

As I knew that he had for more than a year been translating Virgil and for much longer Caesar, I was rather surprised by the assertion but of course I did not contradict him.

I am glad to find Winston today much more composed, and I think he will soon recover from the excitement.

He had a severe attack of sickness after we left Harrow and we only reached Victoria in time for the 7.5 o'clock train.

If Mr Welldon would allow him to try again on the 18th April, I believe that Winston would do himself more justice; but I think the permission would be difficult to obtain.

Believe me very truly yours
Charlotte Thomson

[handwritten] 29 & 30 Brunswick Rd. Brighton 16 March/88.

Dearest Mother,

I have passed, but it was far harder than I expected. I had 12 or 13 lines of very very

hard Latin Translation & also Greek Translation No Grammer in which I had hoped to score no French – no History no Geography the only things were Latin & Greek Trans. Latin Prose – 1 or 2 questions in Algebra & Euclid. And a very easy Arithmetic paper in which I scored I think. However I am through, which is the great thing.

I was afraid that I had not passed after the Examination it was so much harder than I had expected in every way. We had luncheon with the Head Master Mr Weldon, who is very nice. One of the boys fainted in the morning as he was dressing.

The roads were in a horrible condition mud & water & in some places the road was covered with water which reached up to the carriage step and extended for over 200 yrd.

Well, I saw Papa as he may have told you and he told me that I was coming home on the 6th of April. I was not excited before the Examination but felt very (uncomfortable in every way & sick) afterwards. I am very tired now but that does not matter now I know that I have passed. I am longing to go to Harrow it is such a nice place – beautiful view – beautiful situation – good swimming bath – a good Gymnasium – & a Carpentering shop & many other attractions.

You will often be able to come & see me in the summer it is so near London you can drive from Victoria in an hour & 15 minutes or so. they say that the subscription in the summer term amount to 30/- or more & that every boy is supposed to have 2/- a week pocket money.

Mr Weldon's sisters are very nice. I like them very much we talked to them after the Exam.

If my writing is bad you must excuse it as I am telling you a good deal of news.

"My funds are in rather a low condition the Exchequer would bear replenishing."

I am very tired so I must conclude.

With love & kisses I remain, Your loving son
Winston S. Churchill

[handwritten] P.S. please show this Letter to Everest As I am to tired to write any more tonight Winsh——

Winston had undoubtedly been nervous before the examination for which all his education had been preparing him. The lifting of the tension when it was all over may have been responsible for his sickness and extreme tiredness although it is far more likely that the cause of his malaise, and even possibly his less than impressive performance, was the fact that he was incubating mumps. This became evident a few days later.

23 March 1888
Evening

Dearest Mother,

I have, by begging, procured a sheet of writing paper & am writing to ask you to excuse my bad writing in my former letter.

I have bad mumps but *I do hope* I shall be able to come home on the 29th and have Easter at home . . . I am so longing to see you my mummy. I do hope I shall see you on the 29th. It would be nice to have Easter with you. I am sure I shall come home so you had better tell Kate to set about making Hot Cross Buns at once as I'll eat as many as she can make.

Could you send me a little money . . . I am so glad I passed it was such a relief it was fearfully hard.

My mumps are getting smaller every day the very thought of going home is enough to draw them away.

With Love & Kisses I remain, Your loving son
Winston S. Churchill

BOROUGH OF HOVE
SIR
WINSTON
CHURCHILL, K.G.
1874-1965
Prime Minister
Was educated here at
The Misses Thompson's
Preparatory School
1883-1885

Top: Commemorative plaque on 29–30 Brunswick Road with incorrect dates and spelling. It should read 1884–1888 and the Misses Thomson
Above: The house as it is today, over a century later

29 & 30 Brunswick Rd

Brighton,
27/3/88.

Dearest Mother,

Please write soon and say whether I shall be able to come home on Thursday or not. I am looking forward immensely

Four days later he wrote again to his mother pleading for an early return home . . . **Please write soon and say whether I shall be able to come home on Thursday or not. I am looking forward immensely to seeing you.**

As you will not be able to extend my holidays at the other end & the Harrow term is 16 weeks, I hope you will try & let me come home. Anyhow please write & tell me. I want to have Easter with you, tremendously . . .

Evidently Winston succeeded in leaving school earlier than most of the other boys. Nevertheless, on the 4th April he still found himself communicating with his mother by letter . . . **The boys from Brighton come home on Thursday and I wish that I could go and meet them. Bertie Roose is going . . . & wants me to go with him. And I should like to go, but I want to go alone because I don't think Bertie would like Everest – he would think it so babyish . . . I must begin to go out by myself someday . . .**

HARROW 1888–1892

arrow was to give Winston a measure of the independence he was so clearly seeking. His adult recollection of this milestone in his life recorded that the child destined to become Harrow's most famous old boy had been unable to answer a single question in the Latin paper . . . I wrote my name at the top of the page. I wrote down the number of the question "I". After much reflection I put a bracket round it thus "(I)". But thereafter I could not think of anything connected with it that was either relevant or true. Incidentally there arrived from nowhere in particular a blot and several smudges. I gazed for two whole hours at this sad spectacle: and then merciful ushers collected my foolscap with all the others and carried it up to the Headmaster's table. It was from these slender indications of scholarship that Mr Welldon drew the conclusion that I was worthy to pass into Harrow. . . .

Five hundred faces, and all so strange!
Life in front of me – home behind.
I felt like a waif before the wind
Tossed on an ocean of sea and change.
Yet the time may come, as the years go by,
When your heart will thrill
At the thought of the Hill,
And the day that you came so strange and shy.
Harrow song. Traditionally sung at Speech Day by a new boy.

Winston entered Harrow on 17th April 1888 ill-prepared for the biggest challenge of his life so far.

The Thomson sisters, although kind and caring, did not pretend to be a forcing house for the top schools in the country. For one of their pupils to go on to any establishment other than a minor public school was the exception rather than the rule. Thus, on arrival at his new school, Winston had insufficient academic grounding and lacked the discipline and friends he would have acquired had he spent the previous years at

a conventional and more suitable preparatory school.

Winston spent his first year at Harrow in a small boarding house run by Mr H. O. D. Davidson while waiting for a place to become vacant in the Headmaster's House.

Three days after his arrival at Harrow Winston wrote to his mother enthusiastically describing his first efforts at furnishing his room and making what were to become some familiar requests for money and food.

My dear Mamma,
I am writing according to promise. I like everything immensely. I bought a "frouster" the cheapest I could find it was only 3/6 a sort of deck-chair canvas bottom. It is perfectly true that I shall have to have 30/– for subscriptions. Boys generally bring back hampers. I shall not have to find my breakfast . . .
   If you will send me a
      1 Chicken
      3 pots jam
      1 plum cake
   I think that will be all.
   I am afraid I shall want more money . . .
   I will write tomorrow evening to say what form I'm in. It is going to be read out in the speech room tomorrow.
      With Love & kisses
         I remain
            Your loving son
               Winston S. Churchill

The next day Winston wrote to Lady Randolph as promised to tell her his position in the school . . . Though I am in the 3rd 4th just above Harry Sterling I have gained in Arith a place in the 1st div of the 4th very high indeed.

The master said my Entrance paper in arith was *the best.*

Winston must have been pleased to have something good to report to raise his own morale and relieve, in his mother's eyes, the ignominy of his humble placing.

His adult recollection of this event in his life was recorded more simply . . . I was in due course placed in the third, or lowest division of the Fourth, or bottom, Form.

It was from this lowly position in the school and the subsequent pleasure he took in describing it that he himself laid the foundation for the myth that Winston Churchill the schoolboy dunce became the great leader. He was indeed a great leader but dunce he never was. He excelled in those subjects which interested him and ignored those which did not.

One activity which interested him was entered into without delay. He wrote to his mother on the 14th May . . . I joined the Corps as you know & attended

my drills punctually. On Saturday I went with the corps to Rickmansworth & we fought Haileybury it was very exciting.

Winston had not been at Harrow many weeks before he had identified a problem with his name . . . The names of the new boys were printed in the School List in alphabetical order; and as my correct name, Spencer-Churchill, began with an "S", I gained no more advantage from the alphabet than from the wider sphere of letters. I was in fact only two from the bottom of the whole school; and these two, I regret to say, disappeared almost immediately through illness or some other cause. . . .

It was at Bill, Harrow's term for roll call, that Winston felt himself at a disadvantage . . . they file past a Master in the schoolyard and answer one by one. My position was therefore revealed in its somewhat invidious humility . . . Lord Randolph Churchill had only just resigned his position as Leader of the House of Commons and Chancellor of the Exchequer, and he still towered in the fore-

Above: H.O.D. Davison's House

2.

The plan of battle was (as barr as I could make out) the lines

Railway Station for Hatley · *Railway Station for Harrow* · RICKMANS worth Park · Trees central frequists · Breakdown · Harrow rumbles · Roads round · RIVER CHESS

Harrow defends.

3.

As I had not got a uniform I only carried cartridges I carried 100 rounds to give away in the thick of the fight consequently my business enabled me to get a good view of the field. It was most exciting. you could see through the smoke the enemy getting nearer & nearer. We were beaten & forced to retire. There is a whole Holiday on Saturday — try & come down It is such a little way. Ask Papa to come on Saturday as there is a very good Cricket match & I want to show him

front of politics. In consequence large numbers of visitors of both sexes used to wait on the school steps, in order to see me march by; and I frequently heard the irreverent comment, "Why, he's last of all!" . . .

It was to his father that he wrote on 3rd June 1888 hoping to solve this problem . . . I am called, and written Spencer Churchill here and sorted under the S's. I never write myself Spencer Churchill but always Winston S. Churchill. Is it your wish that I should be so called? It is too late to alter it this term but next term I may assume my Proper name. . . .

His wish was not granted. Winston and Jack, who later joined his brother at Harrow, were listed under the S's for all their schooldays.

However, by the time Winston entered the world of politics he had long since dropped Spencer from his

Above: Plan of Action

surname. If it was inconvenient to be at the bottom of the list at school, it was of far greater consequence to be at the bottom of the ballot paper. Especially at a time when it could not be taken for granted that the voter could read.

In spite of his enthusiastic involvement in the activities which interested him, Winston was not to look back on his schooldays as the "happiest days of his life" . . . these years form not only the least agreeable, but the only barren and unhappy period of my life. . . .

There was, however, one aspect of his new life which he remembered with pleasure . . . I enjoyed the Harrow songs. They have an incomparable book of school songs. At intervals we used to gather in the Speech Room or even in our own Houses, and sing these splendid and famous choruses. I believe these songs are the greatest treasure that Harrow possesses. . . .

P.S. I am called, and written Spencer Churchill here + sorted under the S. I never write my self Spencer Churchill. But always Winston S. Churchill.

Is it your wish that I should be so called? It is too late to alter it this term but next term I ˄ may assume my proper name.

Like an ancient river flowing
From the mountain to the sea,
So we follow, coming, going
To the wider Life to be –
  On our course
  From the source
To the wider Life to be!
Here Sir! Here Sir! Here Sir! Here Sir!
  On the top of Harrow Hill,
Here Sir! Here Sir! Here Sir! Here Sir!
  In the windy yard at Bill.
"Here Sir!"   1888

Above: Old Schools, Harrow

Left: Winston at Bill
Below: Winston in uniform

Left: Winston's name carved in the board in the Headmaster's House

Winston did not find it easy to make friends but a memorable encounter at Ducker, Harrow's large outdoor swimming pool, was to lay the foundations for a friendship which was to last for nearly seventy years . . . The school possessed the biggest swimming-bath I had ever seen. It was more like the bend of a river than a bath, and it had two bridges across it. Thither we used to repair for hours at a time, and bask between our dips, eating enormous buns, on the hot asphalt margin. Naturally it was a good joke to come up behind some naked friend, or even enemy, and push him in. I made quite a habit of this with boys of my own size or less. One day when I had been no more than a month in the school, I saw a boy standing in a meditative posture wrapped in a towel on the very brink. He was no bigger than I was, so I thought him fair game. Coming stealthily behind, I pushed him in, holding on to his towel out of humanity, so that it should not get wet . . .

Winston's victim had a clear recollection of the occasion . . . *My first impression of Winston Churchill was characteristically forceful. Standing on the edge of Ducker I suddenly felt myself propelled into the water by a foot in the small of my back, while unseen hands reft me of my towel. I emerged spluttering to see which of my friends had done this, only to meet the gleeful grin of a small, freckled, red-haired boy whom I had never seen before. Glee turned to alarm when I gave chase, and being in those days both swifter and stronger, caught and duly ducked him* . . .

Winston remembered what happened next . . . I soon scrambled out on the other side, and found myself surrounded by an agitated crowd of younger boys. "You're in for it," they said. "Do you know what you have done? It's Amery; he's in the Sixth Form. He is Head of his House; he is champion at Gym; he has got his football colours." They

Above: Ducker

continued to recount his many titles to fame and reverence, and to dilate upon the awful retribution that would fall upon me. I was convulsed not only with terror, but with the guilt of sacrilege. How could I tell his rank when he was in a bath-towel and so small? I determined to apologise immediately. I approached the potentate in lively trepidation. "I am very sorry," I said. "I mistook you for a Fourth Form boy. You are so small." He did not seem at all placated by this; so I added in a most brilliant recovery, "My father, who is a great man, is also small." At this he laughed, and after some general remarks about my "cheek" and how I had better be careful in the future, signified that the incident was closed. . . .

Leo Amery, while serving in 1941 as Secretary of State for India in his former assailant's Wartime Government, reflected on that first encounter. . . *So began the half century of alternate association and divergence in public affairs, but of underlying friendship, upon which we can now look back.*

Winston had similar feelings but expressed them differently . . . I have been fortunate to see a good deal more of him, in times when three years difference in age is not so important as it is at school. . . .

The disparity in their ages did not, however, deter Winston and Leo Amery from joining forces to oil the wheels of academic progress . . . I found an admirable method of learning my Latin translations . . . I formed an alliance with a boy in the Sixth Form. He was very clever and could read Latin as easily as English. Caesar, Ovid, Virgil, Horace and even Martial's epigrams were all the same to him. My daily task was perhaps ten or fifteen lines. This would ordinarily have taken me an hour or an hour and a half to decipher, and then it would probably have been wrong. My friend could in five minutes construe it for me word for word, and once I had seen it exposed, I remembered it firmly. My Sixth-Form friend for his part was almost as much troubled by the English essays he had to write for the Headmaster as I was by these Latin crossword puzzles. We agreed together that he should tell me my Latin translations and that I should do his essays. The arrangement worked admirably. The Latin master seemed quite satisfied with my work, and I had more time to myself in the mornings. On the other hand once a week or so I had to compose the essays of my Sixth-Form friend. . . .

There we'll duck and race and rollick
  And as merry we shall be
As the porpoises that frolic
  In the billows of the sea.
O the effervescing tingle
  How it rushes in the veins!
Till the water seems to mingle
  With the pulses and the brains.
Come away, come away, come away,
  O come away
To the splashing and the spray!
  Come away, O come away!
Ducker is the place today.
Ducker   1887

That small redheaded boy, who first went to Harrow in 1888, returned as Prime Minister on 18th December 1940 during the darkest days of the Second World War. He was accompanied by his old school-friend Leo Amery. Songs were sung in Speech Room and, as always, the repertoire included "Stet Fortuna Domus",

Above: Leo Amery

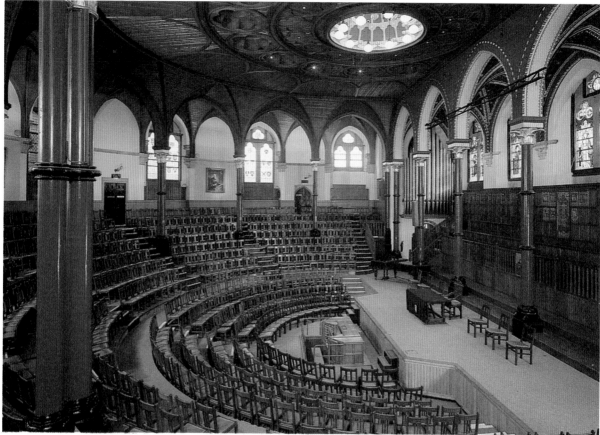

a rousing song which celebrated
". . . the Good and Great
Who trod the Hill before us."
To this a new verse had been added in Winston's honour.

    Nor less we praise in darker days
    The leader of our nation,
And CHURCHILL's name shall win acclaim
    From each new generation.
While in this fight to guard the Right
    Our country you defend, Sir.
Here grim and gay we mean to stay,
    And stick it to the end, Sir.

When the Prime Minister returned the following year for what had now been established as Churchill Songs, he asked that "sterner" be substituted for "darker".

Above: Winston Churchill, Jack Churchill and Leo Amery at Harrow

Winston had few recorded achievements at Harrow but the first of these took place during his first term. He wrote to Lord Randolph on 3rd June . . . I am learning 1000 lines of Macaulay for a prize I know 600 at present.

Anyone who likes to take the trouble to learn them can get one, as there is no limit to the prizes . . .

& No sooner had he learned a thousand lines than he discovered that it was twelve hundred that were required. He succeeded and remembered the occasion with pride . . . It was thought incongruous that while I apparently stagnated in the lowest form, I should gain a prize open to the whole school for reciting to the Headmaster twelve hundred lines of Macaulay's "Lays of Ancient Rome" without making a single mistake . . .

It was all stirring stuff and likely that verse twenty-seven in particular caught the imagination of the young boy who was surely casting himself in the role of the heroic Captain of the Gate.

Then out spake brave Horatius
The Captain of the Gate:
"To every man upon this earth
Death cometh soon or late:
And how can man die better
Than facing fearful odds,
For the ashes of his Fathers,
And the temples of his Gods."

Not many years were to pass before Winston would himself face "fearful odds" and demonstrate his own bravery for all the world to see.

The twelve hundred lines successfully recited, Winston turned his attention to his appearance. He wrote to his mother asking her to send Mrs Everest to Harrow with suitable clothes for his moment of glory . . . I am going up to get my prize in speech-Room on Monday night at about 6 o'clock – Now I want my best trousers & jacket & waistcoat, because I cannot go up untidily . . .

This is the first indication that Winston paid any attention to his wardrobe. Throughout his adult life he was to have a sense of occasion as far as clothes were concerned. He enjoyed wearing all the different uniforms to which he became entitled, amassed a large collection of hats, and during the war invented his famous siren suit which was the precursor of today's jump suit.

Above: . . . I want my best trousers & jacket & waistcoat . . .

Despite Winston's dedication to Macaulay, Mr Davidson, his housemaster and tutor, wrote to Lady Randolph giving her a report on the progress of his newest pupil.

Winston, I am sorry to say, has, if anything got worse as the term passed. Constantly late for school, losing his books, . . . he is so regular in his irregularity that I really don't know what to do; and sometimes think he cannot help it. But if he is unable to conquer this slovenliness he will never make a success of a public school. . . . As far as ability goes he ought to be at the top of his form, whereas he is at the bottom . . .

Meanwhile a more optimistic Winston was writing to tell his mother of his achievements . . . I rank as one of the most prominent trebles & am in what is called the nucleus of the choir . . . Of course I am so young that my voice has not yet broke and as trebles are rare I am one of the few.

. . . You will be glad to hear that I have passed in my Recruit Drill Manual Drill and in Shooting – I made 22 out of a possible 25.

. . . I believe, though I am not certain that I have got a "copy". That is to say a prize not given in Speech Room but by the tutor for English History. . . .

Winston was also experimenting with a new writing implement.

P.s. I have got rather a nice I nib it writes so smoothly + is every good for flourishes

Above: H.O.D. Davison

He clearly spent some time practising with his new nib but seemed uncharacteristically lacking in confidence over his artistic efforts . . . **My dearest Mummy I beg your pardon for the scribbling in side but I did not know it was there until I turned over. However Jack may be pleased with it . . .**

The first term at Harrow over, Winston and Jack were sent to one of their favourite holiday places – Ventnor – to the house of Mrs Everest's sister and her husband John Balaam, the prison warder. It was from here on the 2nd August that Winston wrote Lady Randolph a cheerful account of their activities . . . Jackey is very happy and said as he got into bed tonight "Well I think this has been a successful day". I enjoyed myself tremendously, we (that is I & Jack) eat about a ton a day.

. . . We had a good "go" at some raspberries and gooseberries which we picked ourselves & eat.

Everything is very Jolly & nice.

During the second term, Lady Randolph promised to visit Winston at the end of October. He replied in a state of high excitement at the idea of seeing her and no doubt at the opportunity to show off his beautiful mother to the other boys.

My dearest Mother,

I have just read your letter & am delighted to hear you are coming. I will be specially got up for the occasion. "Nails, teeth, clothes, hair, boots, & person well brushed." . . .

With love & kisses I remain Your brushed & affectionate son

Winston S. Churchill

The visit went well and Winston wrote to his father . . . Mamma came to see me yesterday. I enjoyed her visit very much . . . Do you think there is any chance of your coming to see me this term?

The Rifle Corps had a grand Sham fight yesterday which Mamma saw. Harrow versus Haileybury & Cambridge. Harrow won – we defended the town successfully for 2 hours. I am going to learn 1000 lines of Shakespeare this term for the Prize. I hope I shall get it.

. . . I hope you will come down and see me sometime this term.

Hoping to see you on Saturday, I remain, Your Loving Son.

Winston S. Churchill

In spending two hours on an October afternoon watching schoolboy military manoeuvres, Lady Randolph was clearly trying to please her son.

Opposite: Pencil sketch of Winston by John Tenniel

Winston's next major effort after his success at learning Macaulay was to work for the Shakespeare Prize. On 23rd October he wrote to his mother . . . I have been working up for the "Shakespere Prizes" very hard . . . I do not "spec" on the prize as there are boys of 17 going in for it. A week later he reported . . . I lost the Shakespeare Prize for the Lower School by 27 marks. I was rather astonished as I beat some twenty boys who were much older than I.

To Lord Randolph he wrote . . . I entered into one of the competitive examinations for knowledge of Shakespeare. We had to learn & work up the notes in Merchant of Venice

Henry VIII

Midsummer Night's Dream

I came 4th for the Lower School among some 25 boys – some of whom were not less than 7 forms above me. I got a hundred marks & the boy who got the prize got 127.

When do you think you will be able to come & see me?

Winston was to wait a very long time before this particular request was granted.

Blessed as he was with an inquiring mind, there was one aspect of life at Harrow that Winston remembered with pleasure. He recorded that visiting lecturers . . . made a great impression on me. To have an exciting story told by someone who is a great authority, especially if he has a magic lantern, is for me the best way of learning . . . Such an occasion, though with an instrument other than a magic lantern, was described in a letter to his mother on 7th November.

. . . On Saturday we had a lecture on the
    "Phonograph"
By "Col Gouraud". It was very amusing he astonished all sober-minded People by singing into the Phonograph

"John Brown Body lies – Mouldy in the grave
And is soul goes marching on
Glory, glory, glory Halleluja"

And the Phonograph spoke it back in a voice that was clearly audible in the "Speech Room". . .

This event made a big impression on Winston at the time and the song was to remain one of his favourites. When, more than half a century later, his funeral service, code-named Operation Hope Not, was being planned, the rousing hymns that he liked so much were chosen. At the State Funeral in St Paul's Cathedral on 30th January 1965 the congregation sang "The Battle Hymn of the Republic" to the same stirring tune that Winston had first heard through the phonograph when Colonel Gouraud sang "John Brown's Body".

Throughout his schooldays Winston was always keen to try his hand at something new. Lady Randolph was a talented musician but her son had not inherited this gift; even so he had attempted to learn the piano and the violin and been a prominent treble in the choir. He had tried for the football and cricket teams without much success. He had collected stamps while at Brighton and now he found during his second term at Harrow that he had time to spare. He wrote to his mother asking to learn carpentry . . . **Will you write to say whether I may join as I have no imployment for odd half hours.**

At the same time he was writing to his father to yet again ask him . . . **When do you think you will be able to come & see me?**

And to Lady Randolph four weeks later on 11th December . . . **I am going to write to Papa tomorrow and try and persuade him to come down** . . .

He continued optimistically . . . **I feel in "working trim" & expect many rises in my position.** . . .

The Christmas holidays were not a big success. Winston wrote to his mother in the first days of 1889 . . . **Rash nearly gone. Get up tomorrow,– tired of bed and slops.– Magic Lantern won't work – am looking forward to the sea – It is unfortunate because immediately I get well The Dr says I ought to go to the seaside, & then I shan't see you at all. My holidays are utterly spoilt** . . . **1 week at the seaside leaves 1 week & that 1 week you will be away. It is an awful pity. I don't know what to do. I think I ought to have it made up to me and go back a week late** . . . **a week would make no difference to any one but you and me.** . . .

In the event, after a healthy holiday at Ventnor with Mrs Everest, he returned to Harrow on the 25th January. He sent a telegram to his nurse, **AM QUITE WELL HAVE GOT MY REMOVE INTO HIGHER CLASS   CHURCHILL**

Lady Randolph was in Paris.

When his mother was too far away to be able to visit him, Winston was perfectly happy getting on with his life. It was when she was within range that he felt she should be paying more attention to him. While she was in Paris he wrote long and cheerful letters to her in which he made endearing remarks . . . **I hope you (& the bonnets) are well & enjoying your "spree on the Continong".** . . .

Despite the convalescent holiday on the Isle of Wight, Winston's health again let him down. He wrote to Lady Randolph . . . **I am still far from well & am in bed because I can hardly stand** . . . **I do not know how the day would have passed without**

"Harrow on the Hill

My darling Mummy,

My 'Remove' I think is pretty certain. I have got a 'Copy' for History Like last term & hope to get another one for Arithmetick. I am all right and working very hard. I am going to write to Papa tomorrow & try to persuade him to come down for 'Cock House match'. I am working up my Bible for the Examination tomorrow morning. I hope to come out 'top' I have come out 'top' in my other & Roman-History Paper.

Woomany. I have had another big poultice on my liver . . .

He recovered sufficiently to take part in a military exercise with the Corps which he described in a letter to his father on 27th March . . . It was great fun. The noise was tremendous . . . We were defeated because we were inferior in numbers & not from any want of courage . . .

He also asked Lord Randolph . . . Will you write to Mr Welldon & ask him to take me in next term. He promised to take me in long ago. I am looking forward to going to a big house . . .

Lord Randolph obliged and within a week Mr Welldon replied.

My dear Papa,

I am so sorry to hear of the cold you have had, I hope it is much better now. The weather here is very warm & damp. I have got rather a cold myself.

Will you write to Mr Welldon & ask him to take me in next term He promised to take me in long ago, I am looking forward to a big house.

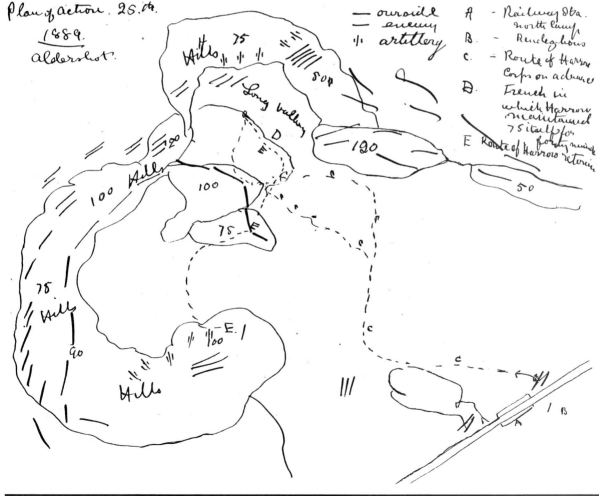

2nd April 1889   *Harrow School*

Dear Lord Randolph,

I can have no hesitation in saying that I will take Winston into my House next term. If I have left him so long as I have in a Small House the reason is only that in Davidson's opinion, and in my own it seemed to be best for him, as he was very much of a child, when he first came, to be under more personal care than can well be given to a boy who is one of a large number. However, as it happens, I told Davidson a fortnight ago that I should like to take him into my own House next Term. He has some great gifts and is, I think, making progress in his work.

It has occurred to me that as you are naturally occupied through the week it would perhaps not be disagreeable to Lady Randolph and yourself to come here from Saturday to Monday some time when Winston is in the House and the weather is warm enough to make life enjoyable. Is there any time in May or June you could come? You would have, if nothing else, at least the opportunity of seeing what Winston's school life is like.

With kind regards, very faithfully yours
J. E. C. Welldon.

In common with others who came into close contact with Winston during his schooldays, the headmaster was able to recognise the potential of the boy in his charge. He also understood his character and the problems involved in moving from the sheltered school at Brunswick Road to the more robust environment of Harrow. By keeping Winston in a small house and not moving him into the Headmaster's House until he was almost old enough to avoid "fagging" – undertaking errands for older boys – Welldon enabled him largely to escape an aspect of school which undoubtedly would have been an extreme aggravation to someone of his nature.

Although no doubt delighted to have as a pupil the son of one of the most distinguished politicians of the time, Welldon, himself an old Etonian like Lord Randolph and a future Bishop of Calcutta, did not compromise his views on parental responsibility. The suggestion that the Churchills should visit that summer was a diplomatic way of rebuking Lord Randolph for letting a year go past without visiting his son. This thinly veiled criticism would not have been lost on Lord Randolph but even so Winston had to wait until the end of the year before his father made his first visit to Harrow.

When Winston moved into the Headmaster's House at the beginning of the summer term, he set about furnishing the room he was sharing with one other boy. On 2nd May he wrote to his mother requesting . . . **Will you tell Woom that I want**

1. **a pair of Blue Rugs**
2. **The Vases she gave me**
3. **My table cloth**
4. **My Draw-cover**
5. **and all my fans**

Left: J.E.C. Welldon
Opposite: View from the Headmaster's House

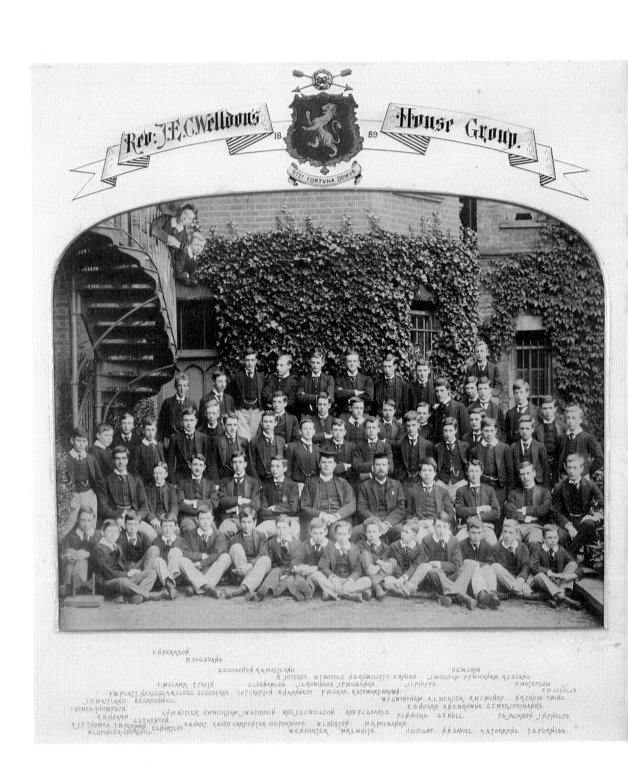

Above: The Headmaster's House

Will you buy me a nice Rocking Chair as there is lots of Room for one. I also want my curtains. . . .

On 15th May he wrote to his father thanking him for . . . the money to buy the Bicycle . . . and asking him as usual . . . Do come & see me soon. . . .

Three weeks later, feeling somewhat aggrieved not to have received a visit, he wrote to Lady Randolph in a more imploring tone . . .

Please dodo dodo dodo do come to to Your Loving Son

Winston J. Churchill

The accident-prone Winston had not had his bicycle for much more than a month when on 20th June the headmaster wrote to Lady Randolph . . . *I am sorry to say Winston has fallen off his bicycle and hurt himself . . . The Doctor calls it "slight concussion".* The next day he wrote again enclosing the doctor's report . . . *Mr Churchill had a fall from a bicycle yesterday resulting in a slight concussion of the Brain. He has been put to bed and will require careful watching for a few days – probably he will be all right again in a short time. . . .*

Winston felt very sorry for himself and, surprisingly, although he was forbidden to read, he was apparently allowed to write a number of letters to his mother.

He had, in fact, fallen from a tricycle as he explained in a letter written when he was feeling well enough to joke, punning the word **try**, and to patronise the school authorities. . . . **They made rather a fuss but I suppose it amuses them.** Nevertheless Winston made the most of the incident in the hope of persuading his mother to visit him.

Mrs Everest visited Winston daily, taking letters back to his mother asking her to go and see him. His writing was, as always, a barometer of his mood and well-being.

My dear Mama.

I fell on the Back of My head on Wednesday & my head is aching & has been sore Ever since to come on Sat. Cant write any more With Love

Winston

my dear darling sweet Mummy I am very well – considering. The fact is nothing what ever would have happen'd if I had been on my bicycle but I got on a tricycle to try it (please observe the pun) and as I was used to a bicycle I turned too sharp & so & and then I went

continued overleaf

to sleep " or ever I reached
the bottom "
I feel much better now
But I felt very sick yesterday
& had a bad headache.
They made rather
a fuss but I suppose

it among them.
Thank you so much
for sending ~~Everest~~
down to see me
She was a "great" big
boon.

But I ~~d~~ almost hope to see your face
tomorrow. It is fearfully dull I
mayn't read or anything & nothing
to do but sleep ~~f~~ (grumble))
If you don't come, send Woomany.
In fact I should so like it, if you could
let her come in the morning, whether
you come or not
I know you will think ~~any~~ requests ~~exorbit~~
exorbitant but it is so terrifically
dull to lie & twiddle my
thumbs all day that I hope you
will give the "Amendment" a
"Second Reading"
and ~~so~~ Good ~~Bye~~ bye my dear Mummy
much Love from your
"ennuyéd" winny P.S.

My darling Mummy

Thanks awfully for letting Woom come down to day Both Doctor & Nurse say that they think I shall need a rest. I hope, most excruciatingly that I do come home. Do come tomorrow or if not Send Woom

Good Night [*laugh*] ~~truth~~

much Love Weumey

Winny

Despite addressing Lady Randolph endearingly as **Lamb** she resisted his requests and Mrs Everest continued to shuttle daily between London and Harrow until Winston returned to the normal school routine.

Speech Day came and went and despite many requests both direct . . . **I do hope that both you & Mamma will come as last Speech day nobody came to see me & it was vy dull.**

You have never been to see me & so everything will be new to you . . .
P.S. I shall be awfully disappointed if you don't come
and indirect . . . **Do try and get Papa to come, he has never been . . . hoping that I shall see both you & Papa on Thursday . . .**
still Lord Randolph did not go to Harrow. Although extremely busy it is certain that had he thought it necessary, or perhaps realised how much pleasure it would have given, he could have found the time to make the short journey to visit his son at school. This apparent dereliction of parental attention did not mean that Lord Randolph was not taking an interest in Winston's education.

I am very delighted at the _idea_ of coming home

Temp 97°
Throat Better
WLSC

It was decided when he was still only fourteen years old that his future lay in the Army.

According to Winston this important decision was made as a result of a rare visit by his father to the children's playroom where Winston had a magnificent collection of soldiers.

... The day came when my father himself paid a formal visit of inspection. All the troops were arranged in the correct formation of attack. He spent twenty minutes studying the scene – which was really impressive – with a keen eye and captivating smile. At the end he asked me if I would like to go into the Army. I thought it would be splendid to command an Army, so I said "Yes" at once: and immediately I was taken at my word. ...

Lord Randolph lost no time in writing to Mr Welldon and Winston's fate was sealed. He was blissfully under the illusion that, perhaps for the first time, he had managed to impress his father ... For years I thought my father with his experience and flair had discerned in me the qualities of military genius. But I was told later that he had only come to the conclusion that I was not clever enough to go to the Bar ... the toy soldiers turned the current of my life. Henceforward all my education was directed to passing into Sandhurst, and afterwards to the technical details of the profession of arms. Anything else I had to pick up myself.

Apart from the headmaster, who definitely won his respect, there were other very important influences on Winston's development at Harrow.

Before he had joined the Army Class he had already identified its master, Mr Moriarty, as someone of interest and was spotted eavesdropping on the lesson when he should have been otherwise occupied. Afterwards the small redheaded boy approached Moriarty and began his quest for further information with the gambit, "Sir, I could not help overhearing what you were saying." When his imagination was captured, Winston's thirst for knowledge was unquenchable.

Already while at prep school Winston had discovered the joy of reading books considered beyond his years. It was at Harrow with the English master, Mr Somervell, that the boy who, fifty years later, in the words of President J. F. Kennedy, "mobilised the English Language and sent it into Battle", really mastered and learned to love his mother-tongue ... We were considered such dunces that we could learn only English. Mr Somervell – a most delightful man, to whom my debt is great – was charged with the duty of teaching the stupidest boys the most disregarded thing – namely, to write mere English.

My dear Papa,

I am writing to tell you all about Speech-day. If you take the 11.7 from Baker Street you will get to Harrow at 11.37. I shall meet you at the station, with a fly, if I can get one.

L. M. Moriarty   Robert Somervell

He knew how to do it. He taught it as no one else has ever taught it . . . Thus I got into my bones the essential structure of the ordinary British sentence – which is a noble thing . . . Naturally I am biassed in favour of boys learning English. I would make them all learn English: and then I would let the clever ones learn Latin as an honour, and Greek as a treat. But the only thing I would whip them for is not knowing English. I would whip them hard for that. . . .

Nowhere in his early writing is Winston's subsequent mastery of the English language and feeling for history presaged to more telling effect than in an essay he wrote in 1889 when still only fourteen. The imaginary account of a battle between British and Russian forces also fore-shadowed his life-long fascination with the military and his love of the heroic. It again dispels the notion that he was none too clever. Rather, it is a further demonstra-tion that he would excel at anything which engaged his interest. Mr Somervell, who could not have foreseen the destiny of his pupil, was so impressed with the piece of writing that he preserved it.

The essay, running to some eighteen hundred words with half a dozen sketch-maps, describes the battle as seen through the eyes of Colonel Seymour, an aide-de-camp to the general officer commanding the British troops. Written in the first person, it is undoubtedly the youthful Winston's fantasy of what he himself would have liked to experience.

The account begins in an heroic vein. **Have just got off my horse for a few hours rest, have been out all day reconnoitiring with the staff** . . . The remainder of the first paragraph succinctly sets the scene – a con-voy is about to attempt the relief of a British garrison beleaguered in the Ukrainian city of Kharkhov – and shows both an understanding of military principles and the need for tension in an adventure story . . . **It is dangerous just now to divide a force already so numerically inferior to the enemy but still the Convoy must go** . . .

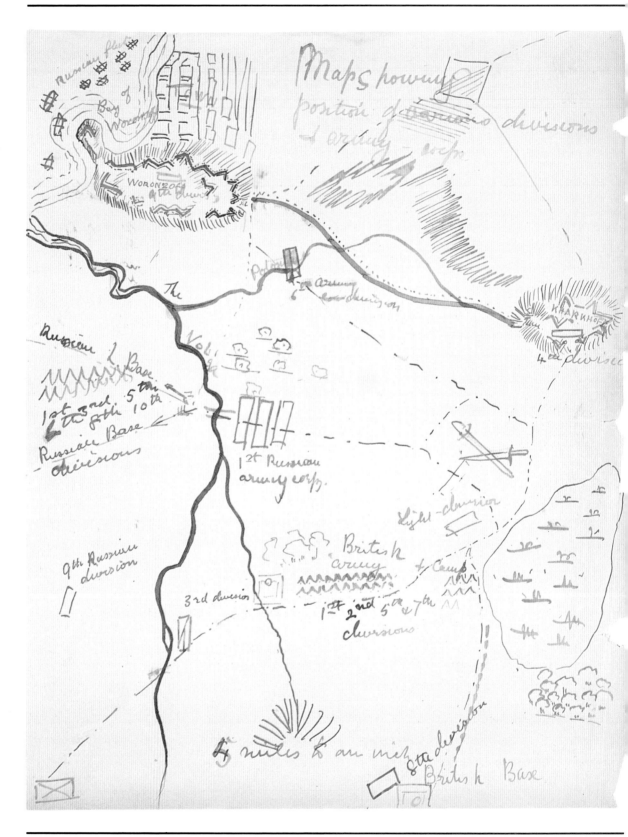

Map showing
position of various divisions
of army — corps

Russian fleet

Bay of Woronzoff

WORONZOFF
9th division

Podol
6th army
corps showing on

KHARKHOF
4th division

The Nol...

Russian Base
1st 3rd 5th
2nd 9th 10th
Russian Base
divisions

1st Russian
army corps.

Light division

9th Russian
division

3rd division

British
army
Camp
1st 2nd 5th & 7th
divisions

4 miles to an inch

8th division
British Base

The next few sentences leave the reader in no doubt of Colonel Seymour's valorous mould . . . **Now I'll wish for a good night as I don't know when I'll get another sleep.**
"Man *may* work
But man *must* sleep"
Though he may be sh—— Well no unpleasant thoughts shall rob me of rest.

Then at 4.30 a.m. the following morning . . . Am off to the front. Heaven knows when ! I'll continue these memoirs.

Winston's knowledge of military formations is apparent when Colonel Seymour joins the General and observes the Russian advance . . . **The scene was magnificent. on the right could just be seen Mt Kharkhoff & its grim embattlements; In front our Cavalry, 700 close by as a reserve, & ½ mile ahead the whole force with 3 Batteries Royal Horse Artillery.**

Beyond those in turn were seen (Les Cossaques) the dark clouds of Russian Lancers. And far in rear of these the greenfields were gray with the advancing mass of Russian infantry.

The left was relieved by the moving lines & columns of red surmounted by the glimmering bayonet . . . dark bodies of Riflemen . . . huge Bearskins of the Guards.

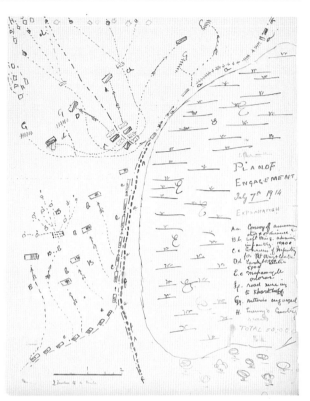

Winston's fertile imagination had been tempered by his study of military history . . . **Bang! a puff of smoke has darted from one of their batteries & the report floats down to us on the wind; the Battle has begun . . . from both sides the Cannonade was opened. From where I stood I could see the enemy's shells bursting in the masses of our cavalry killing and wounding dozens of them at a time.**

Colonel Seymour was sent to relay the General's orders . . . I gallopped off . . . I looked over my shoulder . . . a 9lbs shell burst . . . exactly where I had been standing for ½ an hour. "Chance," you say but that was more than chance.

It was getting very warm now, the enemy had 15 or 20 batteries in position, & the stream of wounded to the rear was momentarily increasing . . .

Our Infantry are now moving to the front . . . But Our Cavalry are ordered to retire . . . The 17th Lancers & the 10th & 11th Hussars are ordered to "cover" the "retirement." (I am so vividly impressed with the events of today, that I cannot Keep my pen from running into the "Historic present".) Thus Winston excuses his mixing of tenses but says nothing of his indiscriminate use of capitals, haphazard punctuation and wayward spelling.

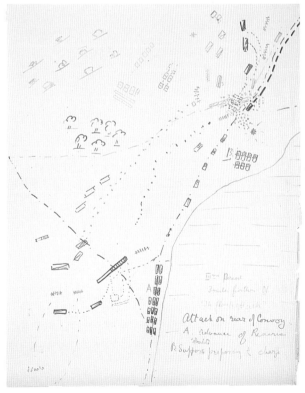

5

The enemy retreated slowly & deliberately at first, but at the river Volga they became broken & our Cavalry, Light & Heavy executed a most Brilliant Charge which completed the confusion.

And thus the 63,000 Russians fled across the Volga in disorder pursued By 6000 Cavalry & 40000 Infantry.

Curious as this may seem it only Illustrates the power of "morale" over troops,

and the superiority of John Bull over the Russian Bear. This victory is acknowledged by all military critics to be Gen. C——— masterpiece, & firmly establishes him at the Head of the long list of Generals which fame

He continues: These 3 splendid Cavalry Regiments charged the horde of "Cossaques", Who performing the usual Russian Cavalry mistake received the charge at the halt. (C.F. Charge of Heavy and Light Cavalry at Balaclava)

Of all the elements on the battlefield none fired the young Winston's imagination more than the cavalry, as can be seen from his description of their part in the action. Within nine years, as a subaltern attached to the 21st Lancers at Omdurman, he was to take part in the last great British cavalry charge and personally experience the grim realities he was now portraying. The British Cavalry . . . bursting through struck the infantry behind . . . the Odessa and Dnieper regiments . . . formed "in line" disdaining "double column" and aided by a Battery of Artillery poured in so awful a volley the remnants of the cavalry were glad to turn and ride back . . . With Heroic Bravery they . . . galop on to our lines . . . The Battle is becoming general . . . a crackle of musketry mixes with the Cannonade . . .

When Colonel Seymour hears the general order, "The Supports will merge on the skirmishing line," the schoolboy demonstrates that he has already, at fourteen, mastered essential tactical commands and the principles behind them. Colonel Seymour is told to ride with the order and Winston vividly describes his gallop through . . . the veil of smoke – through the stream of wounded – over the corpses of the dead . . .

In the subsequent confusion Colonel Seymour joins a battery of artillery . . . the guns were bumping and bouncing over corpses and over wounded men who shrieked in their agony. Winston had been studying the Battle of Waterloo. He continues with a vivid and accurate portrayal of an artillery action. "Artillery halt . . . Action left . . . With shell at 1200 load" . . . The battery is then charged by Cossacks and the appropriate orders are hastily shouted out by the officers of the Battery . . . "With case shot at 100 yards fire . . . Independent firing" . . . I could see the awful effect the case-shot inflicted on the enemy . . . but they were on us their long lances pierced the gunners . . . there was nothing for it but to surrender.

Although relieved of his sword and revolver, Colonel Seymour escapes . . . Seeing my opportunity I jumped on a stray horse and rode for my life. Thud! Thud! Thud! and the hoofs of a Cossack's horse came nearer and nearer behind me.

I glance back – the point of a Cossack lance – ahead – smoke. The Cossack gains on me –

a heavy blow in my back – a crash behind. The thrust strikes my pouch, does not penetrate me. The Cossack has fallen over a corpse. I ride back to our lines in safety.

Further tactical moves lead to the British defeating the more numerous enemy. The narrator ascribes this to the . . . power of "morale" over troops and the superiority of John Bull over the Russian Bear. Winston had already grasped the value of morale. Some sixty years later, when he was Prime Minister during the Second World War, his most successful field commander, Field Marshal Montgomery, endorsed it as the foremost principle of war.

The whole essay, down to Colonel Seymour's final words, I . . . can sleep tonight under the influence of victory which is the best narcotic in the world, has an authentic ring unusual from the pen of someone so young.

The memoirs end with a footnote telling of the author's final valiant action.

Left: The Prime Minister's letter to Sir Donald Somervell, the son of the English master who had preserved the Russia Essay. Sir Donald had donated it to be displayed in the Vaughan Library at Harrow

Despite winning the approval of his English master, Winston's first term in the Army Class did not pass altogether smoothly. He had problems with both his teeth and his eyes which resulted in yet more visits to Harley Street. In spite of these afflictions he threw himself enthusiastically into his new activities and at the end of October wrote proudly to his mother telling her of his latest achievement.

A few years later a new song was added to the school's already rich repertoire in which Brown, who bears a striking resemblance to the young Winston, wins the Spencer Cup.

P.S you will be glad to hear that I won the 200 yrds handicap in shooting on the Rifle range. Position of Bullets out of 7 shots.

(3)

total 25 + 8 handicap. 32 out of 35
I won 6/— it was very useful.
Intend to buy a 'cup!'
W.S.C.

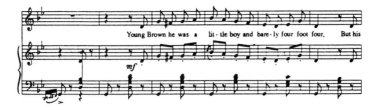

Left! Right!

Young Brown he was a little boy and barely four
    foot four,
But his manly bosom burned to join the Harrow
    Rifle Corps.
So he went to see the Sergeant and he made a grand
    salute,
And he said, says he, "I want to be a Volunteer
    Recruit."

But the Sergeant shook his martial head, and shed
    a martial tear,
"You'll have to go away and grow and come another
    year."
So off he went with grim intent, and did his best
    and grew,
And when the year was over he was nearly five foot two.

Then they stuck him in a uniform, and made him
    learn his drill,
And double hard about the Yard, and up and down
    the Hill.
"Now by my troth," the Sergeant quoth, "If little
    Brown could grow,
He'd make the smartest officer that you did ever know."

And grow he did: and on the range so well he
    practised up,
A "bull" he got, with every shot, and won the
    Spencer Cup.
And when he tried for Sandhurst, he was sure as
    fate to pass,
For wasn't he a member of the Harrow Army Class?

HARROW SCHOOL.

ARMY CLASS.

Candidate for Woolwich Sandhurst   *Spencer-Churchill.*

MATHEMATICS AND DRAWING.	NON-MATHEMATICAL SUBJECTS.	REMARKS.
Mathematics *Has forgotten a good deal but is quickly recovering lost ground. Not brilliant but works well* 7H. J. R.	Latin *Had improved considerably due to fair work — make up schoolwork left. Prose — occasionally quite good for his Division.*	
	French *x fair — works well. L. J. S. Prose — very weak.*	
Geometrical Drawing. *Fred. Has improved very much* 7H. J. R.	*Chemistry: Satisfactory progress. German — but rather slow — latter much trouble.*	
Freehand Drawing *Good progress.*	History *Works very intelligently. Has some knowledge.*	
Tutor's Report. *He has considerable powers of application and is very intelligent. He is getting on nicely.* L. M. M.	House Master's Report. *Excellent* JR. CW	

He also took up fencing, the only sport apart from swimming at which he was to excel during his time at school. This was a pursuit entirely in keeping with his impetuous and romantic nature; in an earlier age Winston would surely have been an impulsive duellist.

His work was deemed unsatisfactory and he had to report weekly to show it, together with his master's comments, to his tutor or to the headmaster. This in Winston's opinion was most unfair and he badgered his mother to take up his cause . . . **I want you to jaw Welldon about keeping me on reports for such a long time . . . and . . . It is a most shameful thing that he should keep me on like this . . and . . . Please don't be afraid of him because he always promises fair & acts in a very different way. You must stick up for me because, if you don't nobody else will.**

Undoubtedly the highlight of the term was when in early November Lord Randolph made his first visit to Harrow.

The Christmas holidays passed uneventfully apart from the fact that Winston caught measles and passed them on to his mother's admirer the dashing Count Kinsky. Their mutual illness laid the foundation for friendship and correspondence between the Austrian diplomat and the fifteen-year-old schoolboy.

Winston launched himself optimistically into the new decade and in January wrote to his mother informing her . . . **I am getting on capitally in my new form & I think I shall come out much higher than I did in the one below it.** He continued . . . **I am very anxious to learn drawing. Papa said he thought singing was a waste of time, so I left the singing class & commenced drawing . . . and . . . I am sure I should get on, as you know I like it. Drawing counts 1200 marks . . . and every mark is useful.** Lord Randolph's advice was sound. Of all the talents and qualities attributed to him it has never been suggested that Winston had an ear for music. His art masters would no doubt have been surprised had they known that their pupil would go on to learn from some of the most famous artists of the period – William Nicholson, Sickert, Lavery, Maze and Orpen – and that his paintings would be exhibited throughout the world and be sold for many thousands of pounds.

By March Winston was able to write to his mother . . . **I am getting on in drawing and I like it very much. I am going to begin shading in Sepia tomorrow. I have been drawing little Landscapes and Bridges and those sort of things.** Between painting his first known oil painting in the summer of 1915, in the garden at Hoe Farm, and his last in 1960, he was

Above: Count Charles Kinsky
Opposite: A lake in Norfolk by Winston S. Churchill
c. 1936

to complete over five hundred canvases including several bridges and many landscapes. When asked why he had such a decided preference for this subject, he replied, Because a tree doesn't complain that I haven't done it justice. Those lessons at Harrow were just the beginning of a passion that was to prove more enduring than any other. Painting provided Winston with relaxation and great solace in times of war and peace all over the world. But this was not enough, as he predicted in *Painting as a Pastime*, the book he wrote on the subject: When I get to heaven I mean to spend a considerable portion of my first million years in painting, and so get to the bottom of the subject.

For the time being Winston amused himself by illustrating some of his letters with witty drawings.

Another pursuit which was to capture Winston's interest and be a pleasure all his life presented itself that summer. Lord Randolph had owned racehorses for several years but it was his black filly, The Abbesse de Jouare, that sparked an enthusiasm for the turf in his son. He followed her fortunes and found in these a way of diverting any parental disappointment at the news that he was not considered ready to sit his preliminary examination for Sandhurst. On the 8th June he sent his father this endearing letter.

My dear Papa,

Thanks awfully. I was quite astounded — Stricken all of a heap in fact! I am not going in for my Preliminary this term as I am not strong enough in Geometrical drawing.

Did you have a rough passage? Thanks for the 2½ stamps. However I don't know your address, so I guess I'll send this to Connaught Place for 1°.

I drank the Abbess's health in Lemon squash & we eat her luck in "straw berry roll". Good Bye.

With greatest love

Believe me

your loving son

Winston S. Churchill

Opposite: Palladian Bridge at Wilton *by Winston S. Churchill c. 1925. Reproduced by gracious permission of Her Majesty the Queen*

The Churchills were not so easily placated and on the 12th June Lady Randolph wrote . . . *You know darling how I hate to find fault with you, but I can't help myself this time . . . Your father is very angry with you for . . . writing an offhand careless letter. Your report is . . . a very bad one . . . Dearest Winston you make me very unhappy – I had built up such hopes about you – & now all is gone. My only consolation is that your conduct is good, & that you are an affectionate son – but your work is an insult to your intelligence . . . Jack comes out at the head of his class every week – notwithstanding his bad eye . . .*

Being compared so unfavourably to the brother more than five years his junior could not have pleased Winston. Jack was by now at Elstree Preparatory School where he was doing well despite having little sight in one eye and as feeble a constitution as Winston's.

A week later Winston replied . . . **I was rather lazy . . . Still there is plenty of time to the end of term and I will Do my very best in what remains . . .**

As was so often the case when things looked as if they were going from bad to worse, Winston retrieved his position with a flash of brilliance. Aroused by the effects of an epidemic of influenza which was sweeping through Europe, Winston put his pen to paper and wrote a poem for which he received a House prize.

The Influenza

I.

Oh how shall I its deeds recount
Or measure the untold amount
    Of ills that it has done
From China's bright Celestial land
E'en to Arabia's thirsty Sand
    It journeyed with the sun.

O'er miles of bleak Siberia's plains
Where Russian exiles toil in chains
    It moved with noiseless tread;
And as it slowly glided by
There followed it across the sky
    The spirits of the dead.

The Ural peaks by it were scaled
And every bar and barrier failed
    To turn it from its way;
Slowly and surely on it came,
Heralded by its awful fame,
    Increasing day by day.

On Moscow's fair and famous town
Where fell the first Napoleon's crown
    It made a direful swoop;
The rich, the poor, the high, the low
Alike the various symptoms know,
    Alike before it droop.

Nor adverse winds, nor floods of rain
Might stay the thrice-accursed bane;
    And with unsparing hand,
Impartial, cruel and severe
It travelled on allied with fear
    And smote the fatherland.

Fair Alsace and forlorn Lorraine,
The cause of bitterness and pain
    In many a Gallic breast,
Receive the vile, insatiate scourge,
And from their towns with it emerge
    And never stay nor rest.

And now Europa groans aloud,
And 'neath the heavy thunder-cloud
    Hushed is both song and dance;
The germs of illness wend their way
To westward each succeeding day
    And enter merry France.

Fair land of Gaul, thy patriots brave
Who fear not death and scorn the grave
    Cannot this foe oppose,
Whose loathsome hand and cruel sting,
Whose poisonous breath and blighted wing
    Full well thy cities know.

In Calais port the illness stays,
As did the French in former days,
    To threaten Freedom's isle;
But now no Nelson could o'erthrow
This cruel, unconquerable foe,
    Nor save us from its guile.

Yet Father Neptune strove right well
To moderate this plague of Hell,
    And thwart it in its course;
And though it passed the streak of brine
And penetrated this thin line,
    It came with broken force.

For though it ravaged far and wide
Both village, town and countryside,
    Its power to kill was o'er;
And with the favouring winds of Spring
(Blest is the time of which I sing)
    It left our native shore.

God shield our Empire from the might
Of war or famine, plague or blight
    And all the power of Hell,
And keep it ever in the hands
Of those who fought 'gainst other lands,
    Who fought and conquered well.

THE HEAD MASTER'S,
HARROW.

My darling Mummas

I have ordered
1 pair of trousers
1 of Knickerbockers.
1 Jacket & 1 Waistcoat
all of the same Stuff .
I enclose a pattern

They have not yet begun
to make it so you can
change it if you wish .
they fully understand the
making of Knee Breeks.

made into [sketch] &
also do to wear on
Sunday [sketch] with
Etons - it also looks right
well when [sketch] the
Jacket Waist coat & trousers
are worn .

size [sketch] & Baggy
over knee

it is one which will
look very well when

Having ended the summer term preoccupied by the
cut and cloth of his new suit, Winston, when he
returned to Harrow in September, turned his mind to
the decoration of the room he was sharing with another
boy.

The illustrations on his letters depict the young Harrovian at the station in his best clothes and in his everyday uniform running to lessons through the rain. The letter M is completed by a picture of the birch, the instrument of corporal punishment, and the birching stool where the offender received his beating.

Did Winston have a premonition of what was to come? Within a month he was to be given the first of the two floggings he received during his time at Harrow. "Seven strokes for cutting extra school."

THE HEAD MASTER'S,

HARROW.

My dear
Mamma

I am quite well & settling down

all right. How are you enjoying

yourself in Scotland. Please write

& tell me all about yourself.

I am making my room very pretty

& 'chic' with lots of Silk "draper'ies''

We want it to be the prettiest room

It is hard to conjure up a picture of Winston in later years without the inevitable cigar. He, like most children, had without doubt been experimenting with his parents' cigarettes. In an age when there was no knowledge of the health hazard resulting from tar and nicotine, Lady Randolph's reaction on discovering that her son had acquired this habit was one of maternal irritation. She wrote to him on 19th September: *Darling Winston I hope you will try & not smoke. If you only knew how foolish and silly you look doing it you wd give it up, at least for a few years. If you will give it up & work hard this term to pass yr preliminary I will get Papa to get you a gun & a pony . . . I want you so much to get on. Don't forget to brush yr teeth! . . .*

Winston responded by return of post agreeing without demur to his mother's request and giving her news of Jack in a way which clearly indicates his protective affection for his young brother. The drawing of the figure as straight as a ramrod was in response to Lady Randolph's constant complaints that Winston slouched.

Although Alexander Graham Bell had patented the first model in 1876, it was not until much later that telephones became generally used. The volume of correspondence written at that time seems extraordinary today when much of the material that comes through the letter-box is either a circular or an unwelcome missive in a brown envelope. During the first week of the autumn term Winston received letters and advice from all quarters. No sooner had he digested Lady Randolph's letter about smoking, than Lord Randolph wrote . . . *I do hope you will work hard for yr "preliminary". It will be quite a disgrace to yourself & to Harrow if you were to fail . . .*

His grandmother, Frances, Duchess of Marlborough, wrote . . . *Take care of yourself & work well & keep out of scrapes & dont flare up so easily!!!* . . . Another correspondent was Laura, Countess of Wilton. Winston, who did not find it easy to make friends with his own age-group, had clearly endeared himself to Lady Wilton who was a friend of his parents. She wrote to him regularly during his time at Harrow. There was a genuine rapport between the schoolboy and the woman who signed her letters *Yr Deputy Mother*, but for Winston an added attraction must have been the frequent enclosures of money contained in her letters and the generous hampers of food and baskets of oranges which she sent him from time to time.

It had been originally intended that Winston should take the Preliminary Examination for Sandhurst in the summer of 1890 but, since his masters did not consider him likely to pass, the headmaster decided to defer this ordeal until the following November. Winston was much preoccupied both by the prospect of an examination which he was not confident of passing and by a coolness in his mother's attitude towards him. At the beginning of November he wrote to Lady Randolph . . . *I hear you are greatly incensed against me! I am very sorry – But I am hard at work & I am afraid some enemy hath sown tares in your mind. I told you I thought I should not pass my preliminary on account of my being put under a master whom I hated & who returned that hate. Well I complained to Mr W. & he has arranged all things beautifully. I am taught now by masters who take the greatest interest in me & who say I have been working very well . . . If you want to give me a chance please let me know the extent of the evil of which I am accused . . . I am working my very best . . . I cannot do anything more than try . . .*

Lady Randolph apparently took notice of Winston's indignant and wounded letter and went to Harrow on 19th November to see the headmaster, who confirmed

all that Winston had told her. She reported this to her husband and added . . . *now he is with one he likes & works very well with – I thought him looking pale, but he was very nice & full of good resolutions which I trust will last . . .*

Above: Laura, Countess of Wilton

THE HEAD MASTER'S.

HARROW.

Darling Mummy,

One line to tell you I am well — working — happy tho' very tired — I am getting on all right & am learning lots each day.

I have written to Lady Wilton — Papa etc.

I now send you my youttoful love and remain

Your Loving son

Winston S. Churchill

P.S. Send Everest down tomorrow Because She can help me in some work (if convenient)

On 10th December he wrote to his mother . . . Of course I cannot judge whether or not I have passed in this day's exam. But I can tell you that I am very contented with the result.

Last night I thought I would try & see if I could learn up the right map. Therefore I threw all the maps (their names on little scraps on Paper) into my hat & drew out with my eyes shut. New Zealand was the one and New Zealand was the very first question in the Paper. I consider that this is luck . . . Of course I had learnt all about New Zealand. I think I can say I have passed. . . .

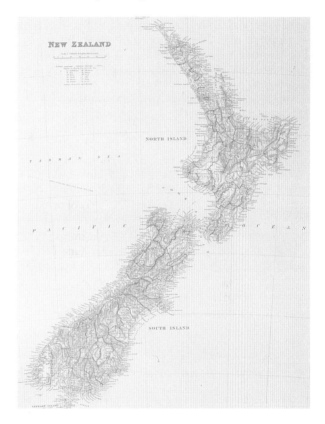

Throughout his adult life Winston enjoyed an occasional flutter at the gaming tables but this was perhaps his most fortuitous gamble. In the light of his own experience he described, some forty years later, how Lady Luck smiled on him that day . . . This is what is called at Monte Carlo an *en plein*, and I ought to have been paid thirty-five times my stake. However, I certainly got paid very high marks for my paper. . . .

The exam behind him, Winston was able to throw himself wholeheartedly into the enjoyment of the Christmas holidays. These were probably the best holidays he and Jack had ever had. That summer Lord and Lady Randolph had taken Banstead, a property near Newmarket convenient for racing. For the first time the boys had a country home of their own where they could run wild and do what they wanted.

Winston lost no time in profiting from all that his new surroundings had to offer and by the end of the first day two letters were on their way to Lady Randolph recounting their activities. Mrs Everest who had as usual accompanied the boys to Banstead, wrote:

My Lady,

We arrived here safely at 3 o'clock yesterday & I am very sorry but I quite forgot to send you a telegram until we had got some way on the road here. I hope you got Master Winston's letter he wrote last evening. They are both so happy & delighted & in towering spirits. Mr Winston walked from Chevely up to the house yesterday & said he left all his bad throat in the train he feels nothing of it. They danced all evening & were out before breakfast this morning & have been out with the keeper the whole morning, killed 5 rabbits & frightened 50 . . . They are so happy & well today . . . It is so much better for them than London . . .

Your ladyship's, obednt servant
E. A. Everest

Winston's letter, though more exuberant, told the same story. After all the years of holidays spent in seaside boarding houses, at Blenheim, or with Mrs Everest's relations on the Isle of Wight, he and Jack were having the time of their life in a place they could call home. The postscript gave the only indication of a cloud on the horizon, another medical problem. This time Winston was having trouble with his nose and was going to have it cauterised.

Before the end of the holidays the good news arrived. Winston had passed. In fact he distinguished himself by passing in all subjects. Of the twenty-nine Harrovians who took the examination, only twelve, including Winston, achieved this. He looked back on this achievement with pride . . . I also succeeded in passing the preliminary examinations for the Army while still at the bottom of the school. This examination seemed to have called forth a very special effort on my part, for many boys far above me in the school failed in it. . . .

It was not just the good fortune of drawing the right map that stacked the odds in Winston's favour. A year later Latin, which in 1890 was an optional subject, became obligatory. Had this been the case when Winston sat the exam the outcome might have been very different. The classics had never been his strong point . . . even as a schoolboy I questioned the aptness of the Classics for the prime structure of our education . . . they told me how Mr Gladstone read Homer for fun, which I thought served him right . . . In all the twelve years I was at school no one ever succeeded in making me write a Latin verse or learn any Greek except the alphabet. This gap in Winston's education was not for want of time or effort on the part of the headmaster. For whatever reason he clearly paid more attention to this particular pupil than was in any way usual . . . Mr Welldon took a friendly interest in me, and knowing that I was weak in the Classics, determined to help me himself. His daily routine was heavy; but he added three times a week

We exist on Onions & Rabbits & other good things. The ferrets are very well & send their love so do the guinea-pig & rabbit I have bought. If I hear the result of my Examination I will wire.

Once more Kissing you Fremann Your loving son Winston S. Churchill

P.S. I wish I had not got to have any nose destroyed! ! !!?! ! ! ! -

THE HEAD MASTER'S.
HARROW

Dear Mummy,

How is poor Grandpapa? I am all right as to my work but I have caught - cold. My Leg has been giving me pain where I strained it, & I am frightened. Tell Everest to make an appointment with McCormack for Tuesday after noon 3·30 or thereabouts. He told me to come & see him every 2 months or so. Give my love to Grandmamma & Auntie Leonie. I have ~~~~~ regularly

a quarter of an hour before evening prayers in which to give me personal tuition. This was a great condescension for the Headmaster, who of course never taught anyone but the monitors and the highest scholars. I was proud of the honour: I shrank from the ordeal ... these evening quarters of an hour with Mr Welldon added considerably to the anxieties of my life. I was much relieved when after nearly a whole term of patient endeavour he desisted from his well-meant but unavailing efforts. . . .

On 26th January Lady Randolph wrote to her husband *. . . I am sure you will be delighted to hear that Winston has passed . . . in everything . . . I think you might make him a present of a gun as a reward . . .*

Winston's frail constitution, which had dogged him throughout his childhood, continued to be a constant preoccupation. Before January was over Winston's nose had been cauterised and he had been in bed with influenza. On 30th January he wrote to Lady Randolph telling her of his fears over a pain in his leg and asking her to arrange an appointment with yet another Harley Street consultant, this time a specialist in hernia surgery. Despite several visits to Sir William MacCormack, the surgical knife was not to be wielded for another sixty years when Winston was successfully operated on for the hernia which had first troubled him at school.

Give my best love to Every one.

I remain with much love

Your affect. son

Winston S.C.

Opposite: Lady Randolph

Winston's dissatisfaction with his physical strength and well-being was a constant feature of his early life. Two years later he was to admit to his mother . . . **I am cursed with so feeble a body, that I can hardly support the fatigues of the day** . . . Perhaps his frailties, playing on his imagination, made "Giants" one of his favourite school songs.

There were wonderful giants of old, you know,
    There were wonderful giants of old;
They grew more mightily, all of a row,
    Than ever was heard or told;
All of them stood their six feet four,
And they threw to a hundred yards or more,
And never were lame or stiff or sore;
And we, – com-par'd to the days of yore,
    Are cast in a pigmy mould.
        For all of we,
        Whoever we be,
Come short of the giants of old, you see.

Winston, who had long since ceased to regard himself as "cast in a pigmy mould", requested this song when he returned to Harrow for Songs on 18th December 1940.

April brought Winston's ongoing problem with his teeth to a climax. On 26th April he wrote to his mother . . . **I have had an awful toothache ever since I got here** . . . **I have not been able to do any work at all** . . . **they will not let me get the Chemist to take it out as they think it would make you angry.** . . .

Two days later Mrs Everest wrote a letter full of sympathy and recommending a surprising remedy.

My poor old Lamb,
*   I am so sorry about your toothache. Poor darling. I went off early this morning 8 o'clock but the Dentist's Man said they were full up & could not possibly give you an appointment before Thursday at 5. Poor old Man – have you tried the heroine [sic] I got you – get a bottle of Elliman's embrocation & rub your face when you go to Bed & tie your sock up over your face, after rubbing for a ¼ of an hour, try it I am sure it will do it good . . .*

                            Your loving
                            old Woom

Darling Mummy,

My Face is swelled up double its natural size through tooth ache. I have made an appointment with Pritchard for Tuesday. I have got some money of my own which you gave me, but want you to send me money money for Tuesday.

2/- 1ᵗˡ Return Fare

2/- Cab There

2/- Cab Back.

6/-

As it will ℍ play old Harry with my Finances to pay this Large sum. I have paid my debts & relinquished Betting.

Winston was again short of funds and wrote to Lady Randolph asking her to send him six shillings for the journey to London . . . As it will play old Harry with my finances to pay this sum. I have paid my debts & relinquished Betting . . . Please send me the "oof" in time . . . He signed himself With love & kisses I remain, Your tooth tormented – but affectionate son.

Lady Randolph, more concerned with oral hygiene than sympathy, replied . . . *I am so sorry to hear you have a toothache, & I hear from Everest that the dentist cannot see you until tomorrow. Perhaps he will pull it out. I don't want to lecture you on the subject – but I am sure if you wld take a little more care of yr teeth you wd not suffer so much. Quite apart from the "pigginess" of not brushing them!* . . .

The tooth saga dragged on through May and on 11th June Winston wrote to tell his mother . . . I think I shall have my tooth taken out on Thursday. I had the abcess lanced the day before yesterday. And two days later . . . Please do come I shall not like going alone at all. The maternal presence was not forthcoming and Winston was accompanied by his aunt, Clara Frewen. On the 19th June he was able to inform his mother . . . I had my tooth out very successfully. I remembered nothing but went to sleep & snored throughout the whole performance. . . .

His toothache may have prevented Winston working but it did not deter him from carrying out one of the most notable pranks of his time at Harrow. He anticipated any parental wrath by telling his mother of the incident without delay . . . I am well and all right, but have just been in the deuce of a row for breaking some windows at a factory. There were 5 of us & only 2 of us were discovered. I was found, with my usual luck, to be one of these 2. I've no doubt Mr Welldon has informed you of the result. . . .

Winston would later observe, with resigned acceptance and an appreciation of his strength of character . . . Everybody threw the blame on me. I have noticed that they nearly always do. I suppose it is because they think I shall be able to bear it best. . . .

To Lord Randolph, who was in South Africa, he was rather more explicit . . . There was rather a row about some broken windows not long ago. I, young Millbank, and three others went out for a walk a week ago and discovered the ruins of a large factory, into which we climbed. Everything was in ruin and decay but some windows yet remained unbroken; we facilitated the progress of time with regard to these, with the result that the watchman complained to Welldon, who having made enquiries and discoveries, "swished" us. . . .

"	Henderson sen	S_2	Repeated lateness	A.J.H	Cane
May 26	Jones (2)	N_3	Idleness after Cane		Flogging (6)
"	Spencer Churchill	N_2	Breaking into premises & doing damage		Flogging (3)
"	Tattersall (2)	S_3	do		Flogging (3)
May 30	Parker sen	V_2	Lying	J.W.W	Sent down to Bottom of Form
"	Pearce	N_2	Throwing stones at trains		Flogging (3)
"	Whittall	NW_1	do		Flogging (3)

Winston, hoping to attract the minimum attention to his misdeeds and avoid too much parental disapproval, casually slipped the information between My hens have had one brood of chickens and laid eighty eggs . . . and . . . I suppose by the time this reaches you you will have slain multitudes of lions and natives.

However, there was no way of placating the headmaster, who on 25th May gave Winston and his partner-in-crime seven strokes for "Breaking into premises and doing damage". The birching, which took place before breakfast in the fourth form room, was the second of the two that Winston received during his time at Harrow.

Lord Randolph had left England in April and spent the rest of the year travelling in South Africa in search of better health and an opportunity to improve the family finances. During this time he and Winston exchanged long letters on a multitude of subjects and embarked on a much closer relationship than they had previously enjoyed.

On 27th May, in addition to news of the chickens, the confession about the glass-breaking incident and the assumption that his father was slaughtering animals and natives, Winston made a request . . . Please don't forget my youthful antelope . . . On 8th June he gave him racing news, details of the latest London scandal, asked for foreign stamps and continued . . . If you have time you might write to me from the land where the Rudyards cease from Kipling and the Haggards ride no more . . . On 27th June Lord Randolph replied . . . You cannot think how pleased I was to get your interesting & well written letter . . . Here I have been examining gold mines & investing money in what I hope will be fortunate undertakings for I expect you & Jack will be a couple of expensive articles to keep as you grow older . . . I am doubtful about being able to bring home a tame antelope. The Bechuanaland stamps I think I can obtain . . .

The gold shares, which were sold to Lord Randolph by Cecil Rhodes at a very advantageous price, should indeed have proved an excellent long-term investment and saved Winston from a life-long preoccupation with money. However, Lord Randolph was not destined to live long enough to see his couple of expensive articles grow up. Following his death, the shares would be sold long before any benefit could be reaped.

On 8th July Winston wrote . . . Have you shot a lion yet? Mind and do not forget my little antelope . . .

Opposite: The Fourth Form Room and Winston's flogging entered in the Punishment Book

On 22nd July . . . I never meant you to bring home a "live" antelope. What I meant was a head for my room. On 27th September . . . I wish you had taken me. What fun I should have had. Have you shot my little antelope yet? . . . I hear the horrid Boers are incensed with you. It would have been much wiser, if you had waited till you came back before you "slanged the beggars". Have You Found a Gold Mine? What beautiful diamonds those were you sent Mamma! Please don't forget my stamps . . . Please bring home the Pointer and also the pony if you can . . .

By now Winston had begun to accept that his mother was not going to drop everything, or indeed anything, to respond to his demands, however reasonable.

On 29th June he wrote . . . It was a pity you could not come to see me on Sat. I did not expect you & so was not disappointed . . .

A few days later . . . I wish you would try & get someone to come down here on Speech Day. I suppose Grandmamma Duchess could not come . . . Try and get Auntie Clara to come if no inconvenience to her. Do get someone as I shall be awfully "out of it" if no-one comes. Next Thursday is Speech Day . . . Please try and arrange something darling Mummy . . .

To be without a visitor on Speech Day, the most important event in the Harrow calendar, was unthinkable. As well as impassioned pleas to his mother, Winston invited Lady Wilton who was also unavailable. The headmaster, no doubt anticipating the disappointment which would be felt by this boy in whom he took such a great personal interest, had himself invited the Duchess but she also refused.

Winston did persuade someone to visit him and on 3rd July he wrote rather pointedly to his mother . . . I managed all right about Speech day (having taken the precaution of writing & telegraphing) . . .

Another high point of the school year, the Eton & Harrow cricket match at Lords, which most parents would make every effort to attend, followed soon after Speech Day and most inconveniently at the busiest moment of the Social Season.

Winston used all his wiles to make Lady Randolph feel guilty for her recent neglect and to do her duty on this occasion. He continued his letter on 3rd July . . . Mummy darling if you knew or had known how much I was looking forward to my "Lords" I am sure you would have endeavoured to avoid that Engagement, or make some provision for my holiday . . . My darling Mummy I am sure you have not been very much troubled about me this term. I

"GRANDOLPH AD LEONES."

ave asked for no visits & I forfeited the pleasure of
eeing you on Speech Day therefore I hope you will
ot disappoint me utterly with regard to July 11th
& 12th . . . Where is everybody? No one has written
o tell me any news for a long time . . . Do try my
Darling Mummy to please your loving son . . .

Two days later his mother replied . . . *Oh! dear
h! dear what an ado!! You silly old boy I did not mean
hat you would have to remain at Harrow only that I cld
ot have you here . . . I shall be at Aunt Clara's. Perhaps
he can put you up too . . .* And the next day . . . *It is
ll right Grandmamma Marlborough will put you & Jack up
riday night . . .*

The same day Winston received a letter from Mrs
verest explaining why he could not go home to Ban-
tead after Lords . . . *Well my dearest the reason Mamma
annot have you home is the house is to be full of visitors for
he race week . . .*

After all these machinations Winston had a memor-
ble weekend which he described to his father . . . I
pent the "Lords Exeat" with Grandmamma in
ondon. I had tremendous fun . . . To Jack he
ent a detailed account of the whole weekend, the
rowning point of which was a visit to the Crystal
alace, with Count Kinsky in his phaeton, to watch
he display put on in honour of the German Emperor.
mong the highlights of the day were . . . **Wild Beasts.**
wonderful never seen anything like them) . . . **Fire
rigade Drill** . . . **Then we had dinner** . . . **Lots
f Champagne which pleased your loving brother
ery much** . . . This is the first indication of what
as to become one of the great pleasures of Winston's
fe. He even called one of his racehorses, Pol Roger,
fter the famous champagne family the head of which,
)dette, became his close friend . . . **The Fire works
ere wonderful** . . . **heads of the Emperor &
mpress** . . . **Count K. drives beautifully & we
assed with our fast pair of horses everything on
ne road** . . .

*Opposite: Lord Randolph's African journey attracted much
nterest in the media*

I must describe the Emperor's uniform. A helmet
of bright Brass surmounted by a white eagle nearly
6 inches high.

A polished steel cuirass & a perfectly white
uniform with high boots. . . .

As the summer holidays approached, a letter from
the headmaster threatened to ruin Winston's treasured
time at Banstead. On 13th July Mr Welldon wrote to
Lady Randolph . . . *Mr Moriarty, the master who takes
care of my Army boys, is very anxious that he should spend
his holidays or a good part of his holidays in France . . . It
will probably be suggested that he should spend some future
holidays in Germany . . . I broke this painful subject to him
in conversation some days ago and I do not doubt it involves
some self sacrifice . . .*

Winston immediately took up his pen in order
to frustrate any plans for him to spend the holidays
abroad. To his mother he wrote on 14th July . . . I
told Papa . . . **that I ought (in Mr W's opinion)
to go but he said "utter nonsense, if you like I'll
get a German scullery maid for Banstead"** . . . **I'm
sure you would not like me to be away the greater part of the holidays with some horrid French
family** . . . **A governess would I am sure answer
all the immediate colloquial requirements** . . . **As
Papa absolutely veto'ed the idea & as I beg you
to let me have a bit of fun.** . . . Lord Randolph,
still in South Africa, could hardly be consulted. In

order to make his point even more strongly Winston added a postscript . . . **Really I feel less keen about the Army every day. I think the church would suit me better. . . .**

A week later the idea of becoming a clergyman appears to have been a passing fancy or more likely a ploy to get his mother to do as he wanted. He was on his way to camp with the Corps and wrote . . . **I have been made a Lance Corporal so I expect to have some fun . . .** To his father he wrote, making no reference to the promised scullery maid . . . **Mr Welldon is doing his best with Mamma to get me sent abroad for the holidays. I hope she will turn a deaf ear. . . .**

Meanwhile Lady Randolph reported to her husband . . . *Welldon wanted me to send the boy abroad for five weeks in a French family . . . After talking to him (Welldon) he thinks a good governess will do as well – and I think so too if I can find the right kind . . .*

Winston had won and wrote to his mother . . . **I am quite well, happy and contented. How sweet!!! I am coming home on Tuesday: Jack on Wednesday Banstead Thursday . . . I can't tell you how happy I am not to go abroad for the holidays. . . .**

It is not possible to over-estimate the joy that these two, seemingly privileged but in fact rootless, children derived from being able to run wild in a place of their own. Jack arrived at Banstead first and wrote to give his brother the most important news . . . *The Den is dirty inside but has withstood the weather well . . . I shall not make much noise for there are a lot of Rabbits in the gras there which has grown very high and we will have a feast. . . .*

The Den was Winston's first building project. He would later go on to construct walls and cottages, lakes and ponds, waterfalls and even a swimming pool. Assisted by the estate workers he erected a hut made of mud and planks. Then Winston and Jack, together with their cousins, transformed it into a fortress with a moat and drawbridge. It was here that Winston commanded his first troops. He marched as many boys as he could muster to the Den, which they defended by firing apples from a large catapult.

To Lord Randolph Winston wrote . . . **Here I am at Banstead leading what to me is an almost ideal existence. . . .**

Lady Randolph was pleased to have her elder son with her after all and wrote to tell her husband that she was making arrangements to get a tutor from Cambridge. She added . . . *He is quite alive to the necessity of working – he has improved very much in looks and is quite sensible now . . .* and at the end of the holidays . . . *They have been happy as kings riding and shooting and lately they have*

had great fun building a house . . .

Mr Welldon, having failed in his attempt to ge Winston to spend his summer holidays in France decided to lose no time in expressing his views o how he thought the Christmas holidays could be pu to the most profitable use. On 21st September he wrot to Lady Randolph . . . *The only condition on which he ca pass into Sandhurst is that he should work hard. Will you l me arrange for his Christmas holiday after careful discussio with my army masters what is best for him? They will prob ably send him to Germany. I should not like to take any ste that you might disapprove. But I promised Lord Randolp that I would spare no effort to get him into the army. . . .*

Winston, unaware that these plans were bein hatched, was more sanguine of his chances and wrot to his mother on 22nd September . . . **I have bee allowed to leave off German & take up Chemistr instead. I am so glad, it means I can safely declar that I will pass next June. . . .**

In spite of her initial good report of the summe holidays, Lady Randolph's recollection of them wa not quite so cheerful after two months in the compan of her adolescent son. She wrote to Lord Randolph o 25th September indicating acceptance and relief tha Winston might spend the next vacation abroad . . . *O the whole he has been a very good boy – but honestly he getting a bit too old for a woman to manage. After all he w be 17 in 2 months and he really requires to be with a man . be hard upon him not spending his holiday Of course it will at home – but after all I shall not know what to do with hi . . . He is just at the "ugly" stage. – slouchy and tiresom . . .* Without the support of his mother, Winston wa going to find it extremely difficult to resist the forces authority which were combining to decide his fate.

While others were preoccupied by his academic pr gress, Mrs Everest turned her attention to the moral an spiritual aspects of Winston's life. On 28th Septemb she wrote . . . *I hope you will try & work well dearest th term to please His Lordship on his return & your Mamm has given you every pleasure & indulgence she could the holidays so I am sure you will try & do your best to plea them & disappoint some of your relations who prophesy future of profligacy for you. I trust you will be kept fro all evil and temptation. I will pray for you & don't forg to pray hourly to be kept my sweet precious dear Boy. . . .*

As ever in search of a new interest, Winsto decided that he wanted to have a dog. The bo were not allowed to keep animals at Harrow but th was something that was unlikely to deter him once h mind was made up. He did, however, need his mother blessing to a scheme which would undoubtedly enta some expense. Fortunately for Winston, Lady Randolp had been negligent in replying to his letters and he was therefore able to turn this omission to his own advantage and play on her conscience. In the last week of September he wrote . . . **Why have you not written to me, as you said you would, in answer to my 3 letters! I think it is very unkind of you . . . I suppose you are too busy with your "race party" & so have not time to send me a line. . . .** And a few days later he increased the pressure . . . **Oho! Aha! What did you say? Every letter I wrote – eh? You would answer – was it not so? And now behold I have written 3 long epistles & not one single SOLITARY LINE have I recd . . .** Then comes the real purpose of the letter . . . **I am going to sell my bicycle for a Bull-dog. I have known him some time & he is very tame & affectionate . . . He is a celebrated blood dog & worth a £10 . . . My bicycle is no good to me now I am too big for it . . . So please write my mummy & give your gracious consent . . . Good bye my bird. . . .**

It is the familiarity of expression in letters like this which clearly indicates a much more relaxed relationship between mother and son than might have been expected in the upper classes at that time. Lady Randolph, being American, was less formal than her English counterparts. It is inconceivable that the sort of Englishwoman considered suitable to marry the son of a duke would have allowed herself to be harangued in such a way by her son or permitted such an endearment as **my bird**.

Lady Randolph replied on 29th September . . . *Do as you like about yr bicycle but it wld be wiser I think to keep it – a dog is sometimes a nuisance. . . .*

Winston lost no time in seizing the opportunity and wrote by return of post . . . **With your permission I will get the Bull-dog. . . .**

Mrs Everest was not impressed . . . *what on earth is the good of your having a Bull Dog unless it is to keep us all in terror of our lives. . . .*

During the Second World War Winston was frequently portrayed as a bulldog. Being a sentimental man these portrayals of the Prime Minister probably brought back happy memories of his first dog.

He is a celebrated blood dog & worth a £18. I have never had a decent dog of my own & Papa told me he used to have a bulldog at Eton so why not I at Harrow.

HOLDING THE LINE!

As usual the term featured a number of appointments with doctors in Harley Street. Winston saw Mr Maddick for his leg, which was still troubling him, and Sir William McCormack for the persistent hernia problem. These visits were by now a matter of routine and very often a welcome outing from school.

Winston never had enough money and was either extremely extravagant or kept very short by his parents. Certainly they did not have confidence in him financially as every time there was an unforeseen expense he had to apply for more funds. Perhaps if he had been given more responsibility for his everyday requirements he might have been more financially aware.

My darling Mummy,

I went up to town to see Maddick on Tuesday I am going again next Tuesday to see McCormack who has returned this will be final. I saw Everest who is not nearly so ill as you think and who prepared a noble tea for me.

I hope you won't be sick but I really must send in my account'

for my journey up to town.

"Dr. to Mr W. Churchill

To 1 First Return Ticket		2/-
To Hansoms used for conveyance		4/6
To 1. Peach (devoured with joy)		9⁰
To Cheap Literature		3⁰
Total		7/6

An Early Settlement will greatly oblige.

I have had. 1 doz photographs of my self taken and will send you one

Good by e my darling mummy. Reminding you of your promise

I remain

Your loving son

Winston S Churchill

Mrs Everest was an avid correspondent but very naturally liked sometimes to receive a reply. On 2nd November she wrote . . . *I suppose as I have not heard from you all your wants are supplied . . . will you kindly favour me with a few lines. Out of sight out of mind with Winny* . . . Winston's instant and loving response must have pleased his nurse.

2 Connaught Place
Nov: 2nd

My dear Winny
I suppose as I have not heard from you all your wants are supplied. I think you might have had the politeness & good manners to let me know whether you rec'd the instrument I sent. Is it having made an answer? I have no news to tell you but one request to make that is will you kindly favour me with a few lines. Out of sight out of mind with Winny. Good bye. My Lamb best love to you

ever yours
loving old
W. E. A E

My Photo

Darling old Woom,

I have been very uncommunicative but. I love you so much. Oh ! ! ! ! ! ! ! ! ! ! ! ! ! ! Oh no! I am not going to ask £ or anything except my watch the silver one I want it so badly you can have no idea of the risks of being late I am.

Pull up.

Good bye

Winny.

Lady Randolph had not taken seriously Winston's suggestion that he might take Holy Orders. On 6th November she wrote to Lord Randolph . . . *Winston is going in for his Confirmation. Perhaps it will steady him – Welldon wrote that Winston wished to become a candidate – I am afraid only because it will get him off other work!* . . .

Mrs Everest, on the other hand, took a less cynical approach . . . *I am so glad to hear you are going to be confirmed. When is it to be my angel* . . .

The confirmation took place in the School Chapel. The only time Winston is known to have referred to this event was when in conversation with his cousin Shane Leslie he observed that he . . . **had been confirmed but Communion he had received once and never again.**

It was during this term that for the first time Winston showed that he was aware of the existence of the opposite sex. He was allowed out of school for his aunt's wedding and one week before his seventeenth birthday he wrote to his mother . . . **It was awfully bad luck having to go, just as I was making an impression on the pretty Miss Weaslet. Another 10 minutes and . . . !?**

Ever since September, when Mr Welldon first broached the subject of the Christmas holidays, Winston had been engaged in a running battle with his mother and the headmaster. Fired up by his victory over authority in the summer he was determined to make his inevitable exile to the continent as much to his liking as possible. Lord Randolph was due home from South Africa and Winston wanted to be there when he returned. This and any other reason he could produce was brought into play to plead his case . . . *I must certainly go to France during the holidays, but I beg and pray that you will not send me to a Vile, nasty, fusty, beastly French "Family" . . . It is still worse having to look forward to such a time as you and Welldon seem to be planning out for me next Christmas . . . I shall think it will be very unkind and unnatural of you if you allow him to do me out of my Christmas . . . I have firmly made up my mind not to go abroad till after the 27th . . . I am sure Papa would not turn me away from home at Christmas . . . Please do have a little regard for my happiness . . . I can't help feeling very unhappy about it . . . I am awfully low about it . . . Welldon; he is the cause of all my misfortunes but for him should be looking forward to as nice a holidays, & as merry a Christmas as I have ever had. . . .*

Lady Randolph found it difficult to resist Winston's

Opposite: Harrow School chapel

arguments and was sympathetic to start with but as time wore on she began to lose patience. On 8th December she wrote . . . *I feel for you in every way & can quite understand your anxiety & desire to be at home for Xmas, but apart from other considerations, the tone of your letter is not calculated to make one over lenient . . . When one wants something in this world, it is not by delivering ultimatums that one is likely to get it . . . You can be quite certain my darling that I will decide for what is best, but I tell you frankly that I am going to decide not you . . . I have only read one page of yr letter and I send it back to you – as its style does not please me . . . you won't gain anything by taking this line . . .*

If Lady Randolph had lost her patience, Winston finally lost his cool. Despite allowing himself a breathing space before replying to her letter, he gave vent to his feelings and pent-up grievances as never before.

Although Winston was to lose the war he won the battle. He was to go to France for the allotted time but he did not have to stay with the dreaded "family" in Rouen and instead was to stay at the home of one of the Harrow French masters at Versailles.

P.S/ I send the other letter back that you may peruse it).
Harrow on the Hill

My darling Mummy,

Never would I have believed that you would have been so unkind. I am utterly miserable. That you should refuse to read my letter is most painful to me.

There was nothing in it to give you grounds for rejecting it. I am glad however that I waited 3 hours before answering or I would have sent you something but good. It have startled you. I can't tell you how wretched you have made me feel.

for your not reading it. I expect you were too busy with your parties and arrangements for Christmas. I comfort myself by this. As to the style — it was rather good. A letter of mine to the Harrovian has recently been accepted & pronounced 'good'.

— instead of doing everything to make me happy you goes and 'cut the ground away from under my feet' like that. Oh my Mummy!

I made up my mind I would write no letter to you of any length in future as in my letters length I can perceive a

IMPORTANT.

READ THIS.

I have got to tell you

that the Frenchman wants to know what time he can come & see you on Tuesday Friday. Please let me know by return of post, or tell Everest to if you feel very 'spiteful'.

Darling Mummy⁶ — I am so unhappy but if you don't read this letter it will be the last you'll have the trouble to send back.

I think you might keep your promise to me + write to W. Likely he'od let me for is n't it? (on my own recomendation)

If you don't — I refuse to go to Paris till Tuesday. Though you will Probably be so unkind that I shall be glad to get away.

7.

I am more unhappy than I can possibly say. Your unkindness has relieved me however from all feelings of duty. I too can forget. Darling mamma if you want me to do anything for you, especially so great a sacrifice don't be so cruel to
Your loving son
Winny.

This outburst was followed by a contrite note the next day ... Please don't be so unkind ... I am very unhappy ... Do be kind to your Loving son ... This drew no response from Lady Randolph who reported to her husband, who was by this time on his way home ... *I can't tell you what trouble I have had with Winston this last fortnight he has bombarded me with letters, cursing his fate and everyone ... he makes as much fuss as tho' he were going to Australia for 2 years ...*

Winston travelled to France with Mr Minssen, the French master with whose family he was staying. On 22nd December he wrote to his mother from Versailles describing the rigours of a standard of travel hitherto unknown to him ... **We travelled 2nd classe but notwithstanding a horrible smell of Brandy & beer on the boat, I was not sick ... Fatigue, the passage, The strange food, The cold, home sickness, the thoughts of what was behind & what before nearly caused me to write a letter which would have been painful to you ... The food is very queer ... There is wine & beer to drink ... I have already made great progress in French. I begin to think in it ...**

Although he received a telegram and a letter from his mother within the first week of his arrival this did not stop Winston complaining to her . . . **It seems to me that with you "out of sight is out of mind" indeed. Not a line from anybody** . . . As usual Winston was exaggerating. Both Jack and Mrs Everest kept him informed of the news from home. The old nurse, concerned as ever about his health, advised her "Lamb" . . . *If you feel sick or feverish or stomach out of order get a Bottle of Eno fruit salt & take a teaspoon full in water. I should buy plenty of fruit eat if I were you keep you regular you know dear.*

If the New Year card that Winston sent from France was any indication of his life-style, he may well have heeded Mrs Everest's advice and bought a bottle of fruit salts.

Winston's letters, in spite of constant references to the date of his departure, clearly indicate that he did in fact enjoy his time in France. He was invited out by various friends of his parents. One of these, Baron Hirsch, found an unusual way of entertaining his schoolboy guest. Winston wrote to his mother . . . **He took me to the morgue. I was much interested. Only 3 Macabres – not a good bag . . .**

Understandably one event that Winston minded missing was the return of Lord Randolph from South Africa after an absence of nine months. Jack wrote giving him a detailed description of the event including his father's new beard.

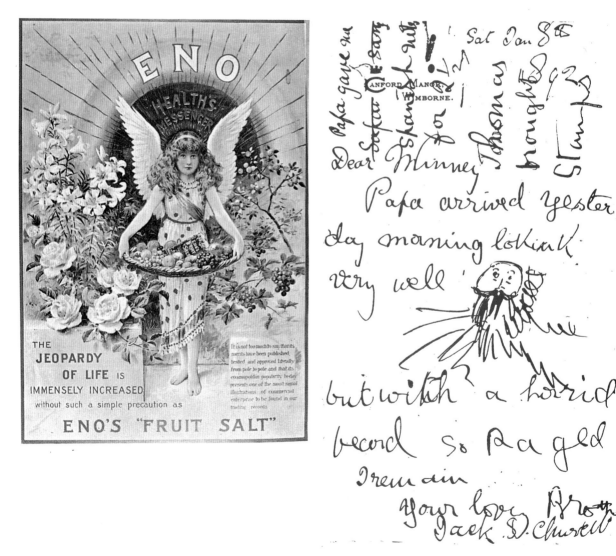

With Best wishishes for
Good dinners on New Year's
Eve + through the year.

Winston returned to Harrow at the end of January for a term which was as usual punctuated by visits to members of the medical profession. This time, apart from the continuous problem with his teeth, he was troubled by his eyes which he complained . . . **are getting very weak and I think I really ought to see a man . . .** the man was seen and Winston reported . . . **My eyes are alright, though I have to wear glasses when doing fine work . . .**

Winston, who as Chancellor of the Exchequer would have charge of the nation's finances, showed no early indication that balancing a budget was his particular strength. As he grew older he found more ways to spend his money and the requests for replenishments to his funds became more frequent. On 7th February he wrote to his mother . . . **I am getting terribly low in my finances. You say I never write for love but always for money. I think you are right but remember that you are my banker and who else have I to write to . . .** This approach paid off and a few days later he wrote . . . **Many thanks for your kind letter and more for your kinder "2 quid" . . .** By 16th March he was again in need of funds and on hearing that Lady Randolph's purse had been stolen at the Casino in Monte Carlo he wrote to commiserate showing an impish sense of humour . . . **I am terrified by hearing that you have been robbed of your purse. C'est Dommage, because at the same moment I must put in a request for un peu plus d'argent . . . Don't go to that Casino. Invest your money in me, its safer . . .** Not wanting to leave any money supply untapped, Winston wrote to his father on 27th March . . . **If you could send me a soverign for myself it would be a great service in making up my accounts . . .** and on the same day to his mother . . . **I'm "stoney". If you could replenish the exchequer it would indeed be Tara-ra boom-de-ay . . .** Lord Randolph replied enclosing a pound and observed . . . *If you were a millionaire you could not be more extravagant . . .* To which Winston responded . . . **You don't know how easily money goes here . . .**

It was during this term that Winston achieved the one major success of his schooldays. At the beginning of term he wrote to his father . . . **I am working hard at my fencing as I hope, with luck to be champion . . .** and to his mother . . . **I am making much progress in my fencing and have beaten the others . . .** and on 16th March . . . **I am awfully excited about the fencing which comes off on Tuesday . . .** and, his confidence waning . . . **I know I shall get beaten yet! . . .** One week later he was able to write . . . **I have won the Fencing. A very fine cup. I was far and away first. Absolutely untouched in the finals. I have written to Papa . . .** Lord Randolph wrote immediately sending his congratulations and £2 . . . *with which you will be able to make a present to yr fencing master . . .* Winston, whose parents had missed most of his childhood achievements – his first ride off the leading rein, his first fish – wrote to thank his father for the money and asked him to go to watch him competing in the Public Schools Fencing Championship at Aldershot. Yet again the horses came between Winston and the presence of his parents. Lord Randolph wrote . . . *I fear I cannot possibly get to Aldershot on the 7th it is Sandown races which I must go to . . .* Perhaps Lord Randolph did not appreciate how much his son would have liked him to be there for this important event. He sent Winston £1, no doubt to lessen the disappointment of his refusal. Winston won and became the Public Schools Fencing Champion. Winston's victory was recorded in the *Harrovian*, the school magazine: his success . . . *was chiefly due to his quick and dashing attack which quite took his opponents by surprise . . . Churchill must be congratulated on his success over all his opponents in the fencing line, many of whom must have been much taller and more formidable than himself.*

Apart from excelling at fencing and being a good shot, Winston the schoolboy was undistinguished both at work and play. However, he was by no means unnoticed, rather the reverse. He was already developing those characteristics which ensured that, wherever he was to go, whatever he was to do, in or out of public office, he would be a force to be reckoned with. His contributions to the *Harrovian*, written under the pen-names of "De Profundis", "Junius Junior" and "Truth", illustrate a trait which became marked in later life, the zest with which he assailed shortcomings of any nature, no matter whose responsibility they might be.

His earliest contribution concerns only the opening hours of the library but within a month, in November 1891, he was suggesting more fundamental reform . . . **The Class rooms provided for several forms are very bad. In some the light is meagrely doled out . . . the wind of heaven has free access from every quarter . . . Either the number of the school should not exceed the number for whom proper accommodation can be provided, or new class rooms should be built. Since that conspicuous, though unsightly edifice, the Music Schools was erected with so much ease I would respectfully suggest the latter alternative. . . .**

His letters ranged widely over school affairs but none with more feeling than one on the gymnasium . . . **I am far from asserting that the Gymnasium**

has gone completely down the hill, but it is no secret that it is going that way. This being so, it is for each and all to see that it goes no further in that direction. . . .

In the same letter he criticises gymnastic activities . . . We have lately been startled by the announcement that the "School Display" would take place . . . everyone will assent when I state that the notice would have been more correct, had it proclaimed that the Aldershot Staff would give a Display . . . In the inimitable prose which was to become so famous, he considered and dismissed as invalid various reasons why boys of proven ability had not performed, before writing . . . It may be urged that no one else was good enough to perform, In that case no further question is necessary. If, out of all who go to the Gymnasium, only five per annum are fit to perform before the School at the Assault, there is obviously a hitch somewhere . . . there is "something rotten in the State of Denmark" . . . It is time there should be a change . . .

Besides shooting and fencing the only other sport in which Winston showed any interest was swimming. He was a member of the team of three boys who won the swimming cup for the Headmaster's House. This was the only high point of the summer term. In spite of spending his Easter holidays being coached by yet another tutor, Winston failed the Entrance Examination for Sandhurst when he sat it in July. This meant that instead of leaving school he would have to return to Harrow to retake it in November. He received a variety of reactions to the results of the exam.

From Mr Moriarty, the Army Class master . . . *I think your marks & place very creditable for your first try . . . I think you will pass all right this winter . . .*

And from the headmaster . . . *Thank you for sending*

Above: The house in Grosvenor Square where the Churchills lived with Lord Randolph's mother, the Dowager Duchess of Marlborough

me your marks . . . I shall have something to say to you about them when we meet . . .

Meanwhile Lord Randolph wrote to his mother . . . *I don't think Winston did particularly well in the army examination . . . If he fails again I shall think about putting him in business . . .*

It is not surprising that Lord Randolph felt some anxiety for Winston's future. The family finances were in such a bad state that the Churchills had moved to Grosvenor Square to live with Lord Randolph's mother, the Dowager Duchess Fanny.

Another sad consequence of the Churchills' diminishing resources was that Banstead had to go. Lord Randolph gave up the lease in October and Winston and Jack lost their haven of freedom and adventure.

In spite of the difference in their age, a good relationship had developed between the two brothers. Jack was still a baby when Winston went to his first disastrous boarding school at Ascot. With his parents so heavily involved both politically and socially the one unchanging factor in Winston's world was the nursery in the shape of Jack and Mrs Everest. It is clear that he felt protective about his young brother and when Jack went to school at Elstree, some eight miles distant from Harrow, Winston on several occasions made the journey to visit him on foot.

It must have been hard for Winston to have a younger brother who, in his parents' eyes, appeared to be performing so much better than he. They lost no opportunity to make unfavourable comparisons between the progress and behaviour of their two sons. This was done not with malice but with the object of spurring Winston on. Happily the affection that the brothers had for each other was not influenced by this approach and as they got older so they grew closer. Meanwhile Winston carried on doing things in his own way.

Winston was young for his age both physically and socially. At Banstead he derived enormous pleasure from organising somewhat juvenile activities, ostensibly for the benefit of Jack and his younger cousins. During this time a bond of common interests was established between the two brothers.

When Jack returned with Winston for his first term at Harrow his older brother took on a protective role. They furnished the room they shared together and Winston kept his parents informed of Jack's progress and wrote proudly . . . **Jack is going on capitally . . . He is I believe the youngest boy in the school . . . Jack has been getting on very well & has come out top in Essay . . . Jack is very happy & has got through his Mathematical examination this morning . . . Jack is getting on alright and expects to come out higher**

this week. He has not had a single line this term, which is quite a "record" . . .

The term at Harrow in their shared room was the longest time they had ever spent together and laid the foundations for the loyal and loving friendship which was to last all their lives.

Probably the greatest sadness of Winston's life was the lack of a close relationship with his father.

Anyone of a superstitious disposition might believe that a curse had been cast on the male descendants of John Churchill. The Churchill women were healthier than their brothers, who had a tendency to die in infancy, and in general outlived them by many more than the expected ten years. In Victorian times, when women were told to "lie back and think of England", large families were produced. There was nothing unusual in a couple having ten children and it was accepted that inevitably some would not survive childhood and that, of those boys who did, a considerable proportion would die for their country before they reached full maturity. In this climate of uncertainty Lord Randolph must have felt the odds stacked heavily against his two sons, both born prematurely and both with frail constitutions, surviving to be a comfort to him in the old age he was himself not destined to enjoy. This fear that they might not reach adulthood may have acted as a deterrent to the development of close bonds.

During Winston's years at school his father rose from political obscurity to be the most popular politician in the country. His various activities combined with the customary remote relationships between Victorian fathers and their offspring did not present the opportunity for them to spend much time in each other's company.

On his resignation as Chancellor of the Exchequer in 1886 Lord Randolph's political career had come to an end, although no one thought this at the time. Despite the relinquishment of office, little time was available for family life. He was still heavily involved in politics which, together with racing and travel, absorbed most of his energies.

Winston longed to make a good impression on his father, perhaps in his anxiety he tried too hard and achieved the opposite result. Uneasy with his own age group, he made the few friends he had at Harrow from the older boys and wistfully remembered visits from Lord Randolph . . . **My greatest friend at Harrow was Jack Milbanke. He was nearly two years my senior . . . When my father came to see me, he used to take us both to luncheon at the King's Head Hotel. I was thrilled to hear them talk, as if they were equals, with the easy assurance of one man of the world** to another. I envied him so much. How I should have loved that sort of relationship with my father! But alas I was only a backward schoolboy and my incursions into the conversation were nearly always awkward or foolish . . .

The last holiday at Banstead was the occasion of an encounter of unique intimacy between father and son . . . Only once did he lift his visor in my sight. This was at our house at Newmarket in the Autumn of 1892. He had reproved me for startling him by firing off a double-barrelled gun at a rabbit which had appeared on the lawn beneath his windows. He had been very angry and disturbed. Understanding at once that I was distressed, he took occasion to reassure me. He explained how old people were not always very considerate towards young people, that they were absorbed in their own affairs and might well speak roughly in sudden annoyance . . . he proceeded to talk to me in the most wonderful and captivating manner about school and going into the Army and the grown-up life which lay beyond. I listened spellbound to this sudden complete departure from his usual reserve, amazed at his intimate comprehension of all my affairs. Then at the end he said, "Do remember things do not always go right with me. My every action is misjudged and every word distorted . . . So make some allowances."

The reason that Winston had returned to Harrow was to re-take the Entrance Examination for Sandhurst at the end of November. On the eve of the exam Mr Welldon wrote a letter to Lord Randolph in order to cover himself in case his pupil did not pass . . . *His work this term has been excellent . . . The two disadvantages under which he lies are that he was not well grounded, when he came here . . . and that he partially wasted the beginning of his public schooldays . . . I should say he has a very fair chance of passing now and is certain to pass in the summer if not now.*

The fact that the headmaster felt the need to hedge his bets could not have given Lord Randolph much confidence in the outcome of the examination Winston was sitting on his eighteenth birthday.

The ordeal over, Winston wrote to his mother showing none of his characteristic optimism and with the arithmetical errors falling in his favour . . . *I feel awfully depressed now that the Exam is over. I did the Chemistry Practical quite correctly and so I shall get good marks . . .* He then turned to the all-important subject of money. . . . *You told me*

Right: Winston's 'leaver' photograph

to write to you and give you an account of the necessary expenses of the term's end.

Here they are —

Tip to Butler	£1. 0. 0.
Char who does the room	10. 0.
To Boot Boy	5. 0.
To the Gymnasium instructors	10. 0. (each)
Total	**£3. 0. 0.**
For myself as pocket money	£1. 0. 0.
For travelling up to London (self and Jack)	10. 0.
Grand Total	**£4. 10. 0.**

I assure you I have only put down such as are inevitable on leaving. Please send it to me as soon as possible as I am in great poverty. . . .

His bags packed and the staff tipped, Winston was ready to close this chapter of his life.

Winston's recollections of his schooldays are almost all gloomy. Some, recorded after the passage of thirty years, are, paradoxically, surprisingly romantic and unrealistic ... **Harrow was a very good school ... most of the boys were very happy ... I was an exception. I would far rather have been apprenticed as a bricklayer's mate, or run errands as a messenger boy, or helped my father to dress the front windows of a grocer's shop. It would have been real; it would have been natural; it would have taught me more; and I should have done it much better. Also I should have got to know my father, which would have been a joy to me ... A boy would like to follow his father in pursuit of food or prey. He would like to be doing serviceable things so far as his utmost strength allowed. He would like to be earning wages however small to** help to keep up the home ... These thoughts were committed to paper when Winston was at a particularly low ebb – the beginning of eleven years in the political wilderness. There is no evidence that he ever had any experience as a messenger or in a grocer's shop but he did learn to be a bricklayer and was proud to show visitors to Chartwell the walls of the kitchen garden **a large part of which I built with my own hands.**

Above: The Kitchen Garden at Chartwell *by Winston S. Churchill 1948*

He did not look back on his time at Harrow as one of achievement . . . many weeks (interspersed with all-too-short holidays) during the whole of which I had enjoyed few gleams of success, in which I had hardly ever been asked to learn anything which seemed of the slightest use or interest, or allowed to play any game which was amusing . . . these years form not only the least agreeable, but the only barren and unhappy period of my life. I was happy as a child with my toys in my nursery. I have been happier every year since I became a man. But this interlude of school makes a sombre grey patch upon the chart of my journey . . . Most of the boys were very happy, and found in its classrooms and upon its playing-fields the greatest distinction they have ever known in life. I can only record the fact that, no doubt through my own shortcomings, I was an exception . . . I was on the whole considerably discouraged by my school days. Except in Fencing . . . I had achieved no distinction. All my contemporaries and even younger boys seemed in every way better adapted to the conditions of our little world. They were far better both at the games and at the lessons. It is not pleasant to feel oneself so completely outclassed and left behind at the very beginning of the race. . . .

Even Winston's departure from Harrow did not follow the normal procedure. As a result of some misdemeanour the headmaster kept Winston back at the end of term. He did not give the customary "Leaving Breakfast" and was seen by a passer-by to "hurriedly enter a cab and leave for the railway station".

It seems strange that the headmaster would have chosen this moment to discipline the departing pupil, especially as Winston recalled . . . I had been surprised on taking leave of Mr Welldon to hear him predict, that I should be able to make my way all right. I have always been very grateful to him for this.

I am all for the Public Schools but I do not want to go there again. . . .

Despite the unhappy memories of his time there, it was to Harrow that Winston went to deliver his first lecture on his experiences in South Africa after his capture by and daring escape from the Boers. How proud he must have been to return to the scene of what he regarded as his failed schooldays and be hailed as a hero in 1900.

Psychologists would surely read something into the fact that he found time to return in 1940, soon after becoming Prime Minister, to sing with the school:

Forty years on, when afar and asunder
　Parted are those who are singing to-day,
When you look back and forgetfully wonder
　What you were like in your work and your play,
Then, it may be, there will often come o'er you,
　Glimpses of notes like the catch of a song –
Visions of boyhood shall float them before you,
　Echoes of dream-land shall bear them along . . .

The eighteen-year-old Winston could hardly have imagined, as he left Harrow after an undistinguished time there, that seventy-two years later on his ninetieth birthday a new generation of boys would be singing a specially written verse to honour their most famous pupil.

Blazoned with honour! For each generation
　You kindled courage to stand and to stay;
You led our fathers to fight for the nation,
　Called "Follow up" and yourself showed the way.
We who were born in the calm after thunder
　Cherish our freedom to think and to do;
If in our turn we forgetfully wonder,
　Yet we'll remember we owe it to you.

SANDHURST 1893–1895

Winston's schooldays were over but his future was still uncertain. The results of his second attempt at the examination, which if successful would secure him a place at Sandhurst, were not due to be released until the middle of January. Banstead having been given up that autumn and the impecunious Churchills sharing the Grosvenor Square house with Duchess Fanny, the Christmas holidays presented the parents of the two active boys with a problem. Lord Randolph went to stay with friends in Ireland while Lady Randolph took the boys to stay with her sister-in-law in Bournemouth. It was there that the accident-prone Winston once again came face to face with death.

On 11th January 1893 *The Times* reported:

The eldest son of Lord and Lady Randolph Churchill, who is staying with his mother and the Dowager Duchess of Marlborough at Branksome Dene, Bournemouth, met with an accident yesterday afternoon. He was climbing a tree, when a branch on which he was standing broke, and he fell some distance to the ground. No bones were broken, but he was very much shaken and bruised. He is in his nineteenth year.

Winston recorded the incident with characteristic drama . . . **My aunt, Lady Wimborne, had lent us her comfortable estate for the winter. Forty or fifty acres of pine forest descended by sandy undulations terminating in cliffs to the smooth beach of the English Channel. It was a small, wild place and through the middle there fell to the sea level a deep cleft called a "chine". Across this "chine" a rustic bridge nearly 50 yards long had been thrown . . . My younger brother aged 12, and a cousin aged 14, proposed to chase me . . . I decided to cross the bridge. Arrived at the centre I saw to my consternation that the pursuers had divided their forces. One stood at each end of the bridge; capture seemed certain. But in a flash there came across me a great project. The chine which the bridge spanned was full of young fir trees. Their slender tops reached to the level of the footway. "Would it not," I asked myself, "be possible to leap on to one of them and slip down the pole-like stem, breaking off each tier of branches as one descended, until the fall was broken?" . . . In a second I had plunged, throwing out my arms to embrace the summit of the fir tree. The argument was correct; the data were absolutely wrong. It was three days before I regained consciousness and more than** three months before I crawled from my bed . . . My mother, summoned by the alarming message of the children, "He jumped over the bridge and he won't speak to us," hurried down with energetic aid and inopportune brandy . . .

Lord Randolph returned instantly from Dublin bringing with him a top London surgeon. In the fall of twenty-nine feet Winston was concussed and had injured a kidney and one of his vertebrae. Winston observed . . . **It was an axiom with my parents that in serious accident or illness the highest medical aid should be invoked, regardless of cost. Eminent specialists stood about my bed, Later on when I could understand again, I was shocked and also flattered to hear of the enormous fees they had been paid . . . For a year I looked at life round a corner . . .**

Although Winston's report somewhat exaggerated the length of time he took to recover, the specialist wrote four weeks later to the family doctor, who had himself saved Winston's life six years earlier, advising caution:

8th February 1893   *17 Harley Street*

My Dear Roose,

I certainly agree with you that young Mr Churchill should not at present return to hard study any more than he should take vigorous exercise. It would be better to wait and see if the albumen will entirely disappear from his brain.

Yours ever
John Rose

Ten days after the accident Winston learned that he had again failed the Sandhurst examination. The fact that he had so recently gained consciousness, and relief that he had survived at all, no doubt tempered his father's reaction to the disappointing result. Mr Welldon, who had remained firmly on the fence in his forecast of the probable outcome, protected his reputation by writing to Winston . . . *you would have passed or would have been on the borderline of passing, if the standard of marks had remained what it was two years ago, and . . . if you make the same progress in the next six months as you made in your last your passing is assured . . . I wish I had got you here . . .*

The headmaster had in fact recommended that Winston should be sent to Jimmy's, a tutorial establishment run by Captain James, a former officer in the Royal

The Grand Hotel, Eastbourne, Limited.

TELEGRAPHIC ADDRESS,
GRAND, EASTBOURNE.

ADDRESS ALL COMMUNICATIONS
TO THE "MANAGER".

HOTEL PRIVATE OMNIBUS
MEETS ALL THE TRAINS.

My dear Churchill,

I see you have met with an accident and are somewhat badly hurt. I am very anxious about you. Will you get your brother to write me a postcard, saying if you are going on all right? I return to Harrow today.

With all good wishes
Sincerely yours,
J. E. C. Welldon
Feb 13 1893

Engineers, to make his third attempt at the Sandhurst exam.

Winston viewed the decision pragmatically when he observed that he was . . . relegated as a forlorn hope to a "crammer". It was said that no-one who was not a congenital idiot could avoid passing thence into the Army . . . he held the Blue Riband among the Crammers . . . Even the very hardest cases could be handled. No absolute guarantee was given, but there would always be far more than a sporting chance . . .

Winston was deemed sufficiently recovered to start at Captain James's at the end of February and true to form was soon at odds with his tutors.

5 Lexham Gardens   *7 March 1893*

Dear Lord Randolph
   I have issued orders for your son to be kept at work and that in future he is to do the full hours. I had to speak to him the other day about his casual manner. I think the boy means well but he is distinctly inclined to be inattentive and to think too much of his abilities . . . he has been rather too much inclined up to the present to teach his instructors instead of endeavouring to learn from them . . . I may give as an instance that he suggested to me that his knowledge of history was such that he did not want any more teaching in it!
   The boy has many good points but what he wants is very firm handling.

Yours very truly
Walter H. James

Above: Duchess Lily

During his time in London Winston had the opportunity to observe the life of his father as never before. Either at his parents' table or while attending debates in the House of Commons, he met or listened to all the political heavyweights of the time – Gladstone, Balfour, Chamberlain, Asquith. While watching events from the sidelines, Winston, unaware of Lord Randolph's failing health, noticed an alteration in his father's performance . . . **As time wore on I could not help feeling that my father's speeches were not as good as they used to be. There were some brilliant successes: yet on the whole he seemed to be hardly holding his own. I hoped of course that I should grow up in time to come to his aid . . .**

Winston's uncle, the eighth duke, had died the year before, making Winston heir presumptive, after Lord Randolph, to the dukedom which had passed to his cousin, Charles. Given the weakness of the male line of the Marlboroughs, less stood between Winston and Blenheim than in a more robust family. Had Charles, who was three years Winston's senior, not produced an heir in 1897, Winston would have become the tenth Duke of Marlborough on his cousin's death in 1934. He might never have become Prime Minister and the history of the world would have unfolded in a very different way.

It was in Brighton staying with his uncle's widow, Duchess Lily, that Winston had spent his time convalescing from his accident and it was to her that he returned to spend the Easter holidays. There was a considerable rapport between aunt and nephew and she wrote to Lord Randolph on 5th April . . . *I am very glad to have Winston with me – for I have grown really fond of the boy. He has lots of good in him – and only needs sometimes to* be corrected, which he always takes so smartly and well . . .

Back at Jimmy's however the reports were not so complimentary and at the end of April Captain James wrote to Lord Randolph expressing the hope that Winston should cease to take so much interest in politics if he wanted to succeed in his third attempt to enter Sandhurst.

On 14th June Winston wrote to his mother . . . **Papa has been very kind to me and Capt James has written to tell him that he thinks I shall pass. I am told his verdict is rarely at fault** . . . On 19th June Captain James wrote once more to Lord Randolph . . . *Without saying your son is a certainty I think he ought to pass this time . . . It would not do to let him know what I think of his chances of success as with his peculiar disposition this might lead him to slacken off. . .*

Winston sat the examination at the end of June but as before he had to wait some weeks before the results were published.

When the results of the exam arrived at the beginning of August, Winston and Jack were in the first stage of a walking tour in Switzerland accompanied by Mr Little their tutor.

Winston had passed. In the history paper he was first by a large margin. However, his overall marks were too low for the 60th Rifles, in which his father wanted him to go, but placed him fourth in the Cavalry list. With his customary enthusiasm he sent telegrams to anyone he thought might be interested informing them of his success. Elated and relieved, there was no thought in Winston's mind that the reaction of his family would be anything but congratulatory.

His aunt and ally, Duchess Lily, was no doubt reflecting Winston's own preferences when she congratulated him both by telegram and letter.

Prospect Hotel
Harrogate
3 August 1893

Dear Winston,

I was so pleased to get your wire today and to know you had "got in"!! Never mind about the infantry: you will love the Cavalry, and when Papa comes back we will get the charger . . .

Your most affect
"Aunt Lily"

Mr Welldon wrote . . . *I cannot help saying how much I rejoice in your success, and how keenly I feel you have deserved it . . .*

Winston was happy . . . **my third attempt achieved a modest success. I qualified for a cavalry cadetship at Sandhurst. The competition for the infantry was keener, as life in the cavalry was so much more expensive. Those who were at the bottom of the list were accordingly offered the easier entry into the cavalry. I was delighted at having passed the examination and even more at the prospect of soldiering on horseback. I had already formed a definite opinion upon the relative advantages of riding and walking. What fun it would be having a horse! Also the uniforms of the cavalry were far more magnificent than those of the Foot. It was therefore in an expansive mood that I wrote to my father . . .**

Lord and Lady Randolph, who were taking the waters in Germany, received the news in a telegram which Winston followed up with a cheerful letter blissfully unaware of his father's mood.

Telegramm N° 353

Büren   Lucerne harrogate   97 15 29 3/8 2 27 n =

LUZERN

| N° | | Worte | Gruppen | Taxworte. |

Aufgegeben den _____ 18 ___ um ___ Uhr ___ Min ___ mitt.

Erhalten von _____ den ___ um ___ Uhr ___ Min ___ mitt.

Eventuelle Angaben

winston churchill esq hotel schweizerhof lucerne switzerland = so pleased and glad you have passed must look out for good horse for you when you return am writing aunt lily =

N 236 with 57. Line 5;—

Bueno per l'Italia
Londra 30 Luglio 94
6585

We, Archibald Philip Earl of

Rosebery, Viscount Rosebery, Viscount Inverkeithing,
Baron Primrose and Dalmeny in the Peerage of Scotland,
Baron Rosebery in the Peerage of the United Kingdom,
a Baronet of Nova Scotia a Member of Her Britannic
Majesty's Most Honourable Privy Council, a Knight of the
Most Noble Order of the Garter, Her Majesty's Principal
Secretary of State for Foreign Affairs, &c. &c. &c.

    Request and require in the Name of
Her Majesty, all those whom it may concern to allow

Winston Leonard Spencer Churchill (British Subject)

travelling on the Continent, accompanied by Jack Strange
Spencer Churchill and John D. G. Little (British Subjects)
to pass freely without let or hindrance, and to afford him   every
assistance and protection of which   he   may stand in need.

Given at the Foreign Office, London, the 31 day of July 1893

Signature of the Bearer.

Rosebery

Schweizerhof Hotel
Lucerne
6 August

Dear Papa,

I was so glad I was able to send you good news on Thursday. I did not expect the list to be published so soon & was starting off in the train, when Little congratulated me on getting in I looked in the paper and found this to be true . . .

At Dover I sent off a lot of telegrams . . .

At Calais we secured an empty first class carriage & travelled very comfortably to Amiens where 5 horrid people got in & stayed with us all night . . . Very uncomfortable it was – 8 people in one carriage.

We changed carriages at Bale and came on here in a coupe.

This is a splendid hotel – lifts, electric light, & fireworks (every Saturday) . . . Lucerne is a lovely place. There are excellent swimming baths, & good food, & magnificent scenery . . . I had a telegram from Duchess Lily saying that she was going to look out for a good horse for me when I return . . . Also a letter.

I talk a lot of French to the waiters etc. Altogether we are enjoying ourselves immensely & I should be very sorry to come back if I were not going to Sandhurst.

Hoping that you are quite well & that the waters suit you

I remain your ever loving son
Winston S.C.

P.S. If you have time to write to us write to Hotel des Couronnes, Brigue.

An intimation from Lady Randolph that the "good news" had not been particularly well received crossed in the post with Winston's letter.

Kissengen
Monday 7th August

Dearest Winston,

We have just received yr letters & are very pleased to think that you are enjoying yrselves – I am glad of course that you have got into Sandhurst but Papa is not very pleased at yr getting in by the skin of yr teeth & missing the Infantry by 18

Opposite: Since there were no passports at this time a laisser-passer was issued to ease the group's progress around Europe

marks. He is not as pleased over yr exploits as you seem to be!

I am sure you must be very happy travelling about & living in the open air. I trust you won't overdo the walking for Jack's sake.

Poor Puss! being so sick. I can sympathize tho' we had a lovely crossing. We are doing the cure most conscientiously & I think it will do Papa a lot of good. Kissingen is a very pretty place – lots of walks and drives. We get up at 6.30!! & go to bed at 9.30 – drink water – take baths & listen to music. The time passes somehow.

Prince Bismark is here & came to see us yesterday. It was very interesting meeting him – I had forgotten that he is 78.

Give Jack my best love – I will write to him next time. Mind you write often & don't forget to write to Grandmama Marlborough. Remember me to Mr Little. I hope his leg will be soon all right. I don't write more about Sandhurst as I know Papa intends to let you know his views!

Best love – & look after yrself & Jack.

Yr loving
Mother

Lord Randolph lost no time in replying to his son's letter. By return of post Winston received a severe rebuke running to over seven hundred words.

Kissingen
9 August 1893

My dear Winston,

I am rather surprised at your tone of exultation over your inclusion in the Sandhurst list. There are two ways of winning in an examination, one creditable the other the reverse. You have unfortunately chosen the latter method, and appear to be much pleased with your success.

The first extremely discreditable feature of your performance was missing the infantry, for in that failure is demonstrated beyond refutation your slovenly happy-go-lucky harum scarum style of work for which you have always been distinguished at your different schools . . .

With all the advantages you had, with all the abilities which you foolishly think yourself to possess & which some of your relations claim for you, with all the efforts that have been made to make your life easy & agreeable & your work neither oppressive or distasteful, this is the grand result that you come up among the 2nd and 3rd rate who are only good for commissions in a cavalry regiment.

The second discreditable fact in the result of your examination is that you have not perceptibly increased as far as my memory serves me the marks you made in the examination, & perhaps even you have decreased them inspite of there being less competition in the last than in the former examination . . . You may find some consolation that you have failed to get into the "60th Rifles" one of the finest regiments in the army. There is another satisfaction for you in that by accomplishing the prodigious effort of getting into the Cavalry, you imposed on me an extra charge of some £200 a year. Not that I shall allow you to remain in the Cavalry. As soon as possible I shall arrange your exchange into an infantry regiment of the line.

Now it is a good thing to put this business vy plainly before you. Do not think I am going to take the trouble of writing to you long letters again on these matters & you need not trouble to write any answer to this part of my letter, because I no longer attach the slightest weight to anything you may say about your own acquirements & exploits . . . if your conduct and action at Sandhurst is similar to what it has been in the other establishments . . . then my responsibility for you is over . . . Because I am certain that if you cannot prevent yourself from leading the idle useless unprofitable life you have had during your schooldays . . . you will become a mere social wastrel one of the hundreds of the public school failures, and you will degenerate into a shabby unhappy & futile existence . . .

I hope you will be better for your trip. You must apply to Capt James for advice for us to your Sandhurst equipment. Your mother sends her love.

Your affte father
Randolph S.C.

Kissingen

GROSVENOR SQUARE
W.   August 9 1893

My dear Winston I am rather surprised at your tone of exultation over your inclusion in the Sandhurst list. There are two ways of winning in an examination one creditable the other the reverse. You have unfortunately chosen the latter method, and appear to be much pleased with your success.

Lord Randolph's reaction was undoubtedly affected by his failing health. He was in the grip of an illness which would prove fatal within eighteen months. In a healthier state of mind he might have glimpsed the signs which, with hindsight, are now obvious. That Winston was far from lazy. That his ability and intellect would better have been judged against the fact that he could excel whenever he chose, rather than by his lack of interest when uninspiring teachers failed to convey the relevance of their subjects.

Unaware of the seriousness of Lord Randolph's illness and thus making no allowance for it, Winston found to his surprise . . . that he took a contrary view . . . He had it seemed already written to the Duke of Cambridge, who was the Colonel-in-Chief of the 60th, suggesting I should ultimately enter his regiment, and had received a gracious response. Now all these plans were upset, and upset in the most inconvenient and expensive manner . . . "In the infantry," my father had remarked, "one has to keep a man; in the cavalry a man and a horse as well." This was not only true, but even an understatement. Little did he foresee not only one horse, but two official chargers and one or two hunters besides – to say nothing of the indispensable string of polo ponies! . . . Despite being . . . pained and startled . . . by his father's unexpected rebuke in his hour of triumph Winston managed to retain his sense of humour and enthusiasm for what was ahead . . . All the same I rejoiced at going to Sandhurst, and at the prospect of becoming a real live cavalry officer in no more than 18 months . . .

In the meantime Winston and Jack, accompanied by Mr Little, the tutor, continued on their walking-tour of Switzerland . . . we travelled by train as far as the money lasted . . . I longed to climb the Matterhorn, but this was not only too expensive but held by the tutor to be too dangerous . . . As always in Winston's early years it was not so much that he went looking for danger but that danger was on the look-out for him and more than happy to meet him half-way. The Matterhorn having evaded him Winston sought amusement on the lake of Lausanne where he . . . went for a row with another boy a little younger than myself. When we were more than a mile from the shore, we decided to have a swim, pulled off our clothes, jumped into the water and swam about in great delight. When we had had enough, the boat was perhaps one hundred yards away. A breeze had begun to stir the waters. The boat had a small red awning . . . This awning acted as a sail . . . As we swam towards the boat, it drifted further off . . . this had

happened several times . . . we both, especially my companion, began to be tired. Up to this point no idea of danger had crossed my mind . . . But now I saw Death as near as I believe I have ever seen him. He was swimming in the water at our side . . . No help was near. Unaided we could never reach the shore . . . I now swam for life. Twice I reached within a yard of the boat and each time a gust carried it just beyond my reach; but by a supreme effort I caught hold of its side in the nick of time . . . I scrambled in, and rowed back for my companion who, though tired, had not apparently realized the dull yellow glare of mortal peril that had so suddenly played around us. I said nothing to the tutor about this serious experience; but I have never forgotten it . . .

At the time Winston would not have wanted to admit that he had led his younger brother in an incident which could so easily have ended in tragedy. However there is no logical reason why more than thirty years later he did not reveal the identity of the other boy who was almost certainly Jack.

Neither his father's bleak letter nor his brush with death was allowed to cloud Winston's horizon as he decided on the party's itinerary. Lord Randolph had appreciated this situation exactly when he wrote on 20th August to his mother . . . *We have heard from the boys . . . I do not at all approve of their having gone down to Italy . . . I expect Winston has overpowered Little & taken the entire command of all the travel arrangements. . . .* Two days later Mr Little was reporting . . . *I am sorry that we did not stick more to Switzerland but . . . Winston was very anxious to see Lugano and Baveno . . . Jack's French improves, but not very rapidly . . . I think he will learn more after Winston's departure; the latter's French is so voluble, that Jack seldom finds himself absolutely forced to speak. . . .*

Above: Lake Scene in Switzerland *by Winston S. Churchill 1945*

There was a constant flow of letters between Lord and Lady Randolph in Germany and the holidaymakers as they continued with their tour. A chastened Winston neatly avoided replying in any detail to any of his father's diatribe . . . I am very sorry indeed that you are displeased with me. As however you tell me not to refer to the part of your letter about the Examination I will not do so, but will try to modify your opinion of me by my work & conduct at Sandhurst . . . I am very sorry indeed that I have done so badly . . .

Simultaneously Winston was writing to his mother.

Hotel Couronne & Poste
Brigue
23 August

Dear Mamma,

Thank you so much for your letter, which I got yesterday at Zermatt. I have written to Papa the account of what we did there. The trip is splendid & we are having such fun . . .

I am going to buckle to at Sandhurst & to try and regain Papa's opinion of me. I will send you a Photograph of myself in my uniform – which I am longing to put on.

When I have been there a day or two I will write you and Papa a long letter & describe everything. I have got a good deal of money in hand (£7) but I don't know at all what my expenses are likely to be on joining & I have had no information. You might suggest an allowance to Papa.

Thanking you once more for your letter and sending you my very best love & many kisses.

I remain Ever your loving son
Winston S.C.

Mr Little meanwhile continued to keep Lord Randolph informed of their travels and of the boys' progress in French. Winston got on well with the tutor, who was clearly in sympathy with him, and it was to him that he confided when he received his father's angry letter. The tutor wrote . . . When he showed me your letter, we had a long talk and he told me a good deal about his views of man and things. He was a good deal depressed . . .

On his return to London Winston found that, because a number of successful candidates had not taken up their vacancies, he had been awarded an infantry cadetship after all. He wrote a long letter to his father discussing the financial aspects of his new life, concluding . . . Hoping you will send me some money for my immediate needs (I don't know what to do if you don't) & you will not be angry for what I have written . . . *Address after Friday* Royal Military College Sandhurst.

Anticipating an adverse reaction to his request for some degree of financial independence, Winston also wrote to his mother.

> 50 Grosvenor Square
> 30 August

Dear Mamma,

I got your letter this morning. You did not say anything about the absorbing topic – money. I have written a long & respectful letter to Papa to ask him to give me an allowance. Please try & persuade him. It would be much better & cheaper than the present arrangements which are

"Spend as much as I can get"

"Get as much as I can".

I have been anxiously awaiting a letter from Papa. But have had none since the one he wrote me on my examination 3 weeks ago. I hope he will be pleased to hear that I have got into the infantry after all.

I had a very tiring journey from Geneva. I stayed 5 hours in Paris – hoping to see the Eiffel Tower but 'twas shut. I went to the Hotel de Louvre & had bath & breakfast. (I wanted both after 18 hours in train.) Then I walked about till it was time to go & so came safely here.

I do not know what I shall do unless I get some money before the 1st proximo. I would have written & asked for some only I expected by every post a letter from Papa. Good-Bye dear Mamma – I will write to you from Sandhurst on Sunday.

> I remain Your Ever loving son
> Winston S.C.

On 31st August Lord Randolph telegraphed Winston that a cheque had been sent to Sandhurst for him.

On 3rd September Lord Randolph wrote to explain his feelings to his mother . . . *I am very glad that Winston has got an infantry cadetship. It will save me £200 a year. I enclose you a letter I received from Winston . . . I told him I would give him £10 a month out of which he would have to pay for small articles of clothing, & for other small necessaries but that I will continue to pay his tailor & haberdasher while he was at Sandhurst . . . I wrote very kindly to him & did not lecture. . . .*

Lord Randolph had a close relationship with his mother and very often took notice of what she said, not however on the subject of his sister-in-law . . . *I don't agree with you about the Duchess Lily being a useful friend to him. I think her very silly & gushing . . .*

Although he could not have doubted that funds would be forthcoming Winston was relieved to have the financial arrangements confirmed, especially as he had already been obliged to equip himself for his new life. On his return from the continent he had thrown himself enthusiastically into . . . **ordering the considerable necessary outfit of a gentleman-cadet.**

POST OFFICE TELEGRAPHS. No. of Telegram.................

If the accuracy of an Inland Telegram be doubted, the telegram will be repeated on payment of half the amount ... ally paid for its transmission, any fraction of 1d. less than ½d. being reckoned as ½d.; and if it be found that there was any inaccuracy, ... amount paid for repetition will be refunded. Special conditions are applicable to the repetition of Foreign Telegrams.

Charges to pay } £ s. d.

Handed in at *Badgastein* Office at Received here at

TO { *Churchill 53 Seymour St West*

Have forwarded Sandhurst papers to you there also sent Cheque for term delay not any fault R. C.

N.B.—This Form must accompany any inquiry made respecting this Telegram.

... At Sandhurst I had a new start. I was no longer handicapped by past neglect of Latin, French or Mathematics. We now had to learn new things and we all started equal ... I did not much like the drill and indeed figured for several months in the "Awkward Squad", formed from those who required special smartening up ... It did seem such a pity that it all had to be make-believe, and that the age of wars between civilized nations had come to an end for ever ...

On 3rd September Winston, who was still waiting for his money, proudly told his father ... *I am very glad to be able to write to you on this extremely smart paper ... At 6.30 Revelly sounds and you have to be dressed by 7 o'clock ... I am very contented and like the place very much – though it is freely said that it "combines the evils of the life of a private schoolboy with those of a private soldier." The room I have with 2 others is very large and divided into cubicles like stalls in a stable ... No hot water and very little cold ... The discipline is extremely strict ... far stricter than Harrow ... The food here is not very good ... Smoking is allowed everywhere ... The dinner is very grand – and the names of the dishes are written in French on the menu. There is nothing else French about them ... Altogether I like the life ... Hoping you will write to me and send me some money ...*

Winston was worried how to pay his bills. His grandmother, Mrs Leonard Jerome, was fearful that he might resort to desperate measures and wrote to him on 4th September ... *You remember the conversation we had about the watch, how easily one could borrow money on it. So I was afraid you might have done so ...*

The next day he was solvent and wrote to Lord Randolph ... *£10 per month will be ample ... Thank you very much for your very generous allowance ...*

No sooner had one problem been resolved, if only temporarily, than another presented itself. Winston wanted permission on two counts: first to go out with whoever he chose and second to be allowed to ride hired horses from the village. As was so often the case Lord Randolph referred the matter to his mother, perhaps in the expectation that she would approve his action whereas his wife would probably have taken a more indulgent line. The Duchess who, despite occasionally taking Winston's side, was at heart a strict disciplinarian, gave her opinion ... *I think you are right to turn a deaf ear ... Still I prefer his open requests & there is one advantage he is very frank and open in his pertinacity. I think the no restriction permission is most objectionable & the request for a Horse unnecessary ... the great thing is for him to feel he is not the son of a rich man ...*

Top: Sandhurst

The awkward squad – "Right turn!" –

Sept. 3

Dear Papa.

I am very glad to be able to write to you on this extremely smart paper. On Friday I left London by the 12·20 & got down here in time for lunch. Since then I have had little or nothing to do. Yesterday there was a drill at 10 o'clock for an hour & to day there has been a parade & church.

The first 3 days are

Top: *One of a series of cartoons by a Sandhurst cadet*
Above: *Uniform of a Gentleman Cadet*
Left: *Winston's first letter home*

Not being able to hire horses was not a problem as there were plenty available at Sandhurst. The withholding of permission for "unrestricted leave" was both inconvenient and humiliating as he explained to his mother . . . it is very hard that Papa cannot grant me the same liberty that other boys in my position are granted. It is only a case of trusting *me*. As my company officer said he "liked to know the boys whom their parents could trust" – and therefore recommended me to get the permission I asked for. However it is no use trying to explain to Papa, & I shall go on being treated as "that boy" till I am 50 years old . . .

In the same letter Winston opened his heart to his mother . . . Your letter arrived last night, and made me feel rather unhappy. I am awfully sorry that Papa does not approve of my letters. I take a great deal of pains over them & often re-write entire pages. If I write a descriptive account of my life here, I receive a hint from you that my style is too sententious & stilted. If on the other hand I write a plain and excessively simple letter – it is put down as slovenly. I can never do anything right . . . The new gentleman-cadet was feeling very hard-done-by but at least with his mother he could be himself . . . It is a great pleasure to me to write to you unreservedly instead of having to pick & choose my words and information . . .

With his history of one medical problem after another and his lack of athletic prowess at school, it would have been astonishing if Winston had found the physical rigours of Sandhurst trouble free. This side of life was to present him with yet another challenge to overcome. On 17th September he wrote to his mother . . . I am cursed with so feeble a body, that I can hardly support the fatigues of the day; but I suppose I shall get stronger during my stay here . . . The drill is progressing and my shoulders are greatly improving . . . On 13th October he again referred to his physical handicaps when writing to Lady Randolph . . . I had to be helped off parade by a couple of sergeants – this was after a run in full equipment – I have been to see the doctor and he says there is nothing wrong except that my heart does not seem very strong. He has given me a tonic & lighter work for a few days . . .

To add to his troubles Winston's skin erupted. He had, in passing, referred to this in a letter to his mother on 20th September . . . I am very well but have a horrid boil or abcess on my left cheek – which gives me great pain & has swollen my face to an abnormal size . . . The boil went as boils do, until

Royal Military College,
Yorktown,
Camberley, Surrey.

I took the Turkish bath. I have been to see the doctor & he says there is nothing wrong except that my heart does not seem very strong.

Goodbye my darling Mummy. Longing to see you.
remain
Ever your loving
Winston S.C.

Opposite: Lady Randolph's favourite portrait of Winston

the next time. Winston consulted the army surgeon, who reassured him with the comforting information that . . . **they were a sign of good health.** This distressing manifestation of "good health" was to become a feature of Winston's time at Sandhurst. The combination of a less than adequate physique and a series of embarrassing eruptions was no asset to a young man trying to cut a dash in his smart new uniform. He would later observe . . . **I admire a manly man but I cannot bear a boily boy.** His play on words no doubt reflected the youthful Winston's agonies over his own physical and cosmetic disadvantages, which together would have sabotaged the self-esteem of many a lesser young man.

Lord Randolph's inconsistent handling of his eldest son was no doubt due largely to his illness and its encroaching effect upon his mind and to his increasing preoccupation with his lack of money. But, whatever the reason, his swings of mood made life difficult for Winston. On the one hand Lord Randolph relented – as far as the college was concerned – and sanctioned unrestricted leave. On the other he maintained a curb on Winston's weekend activities by restricting his visits to London. He often admonished his son as if he was still a small boy, yet delighted in showing Winston off to his own circle, taking him to Lord Rothschild's house at Tring, where the leading lights of the Conservative Party often gathered, to stay with his racing friends and even to the circus.

While staying at Tring, Winston wrote to his mother on 21st October . . . **Papa was very pleased to see me and talked to me for quite a long time about his speeches & my prospects. . . .** A week earlier Lord Randolph had persuaded the Duke of Cambridge, the Commander-in-Chief of the Army, to agree that Winston would be commissioned into the 60th Rifles.

At the same time Lord Randolph was writing well of Winston to his mother . . . *He has much smartened up . . . he has got steadier. The people at Tring took a great deal of notice of him . . .* There was also recognition that Winston's monthly allowance was inadequate . . . *I paid his mess bill for him £6 so that his next allowance might no be "empiété" upon. I think he deserved it . . .*

The Churchills' finances were going from bad to worse. Lord Randolph's concern at the added expense of maintaining Winston in a cavalry regiment was not without foundation. On 6th October he had to write to Lady Randolph who was in Paris and in need of money . . . *Dearest I am very sorry but I have no money at the present moment & balance overdrawn at bank . . . I will try & send you £105 . . .* Winston, whose needs and desires were easily satisfied by the odd ten-pound tip for which he had several sources, was undoubtedly unaware of the

Right: Prescription for a tonic

precarious state of his parents' finances.

At last he was, at least some of the time, being treated like a grown-up . . . Once I became a gentleman-cadet I acquired a new status in my father's eyes. I was entitled when on leave to go about with him . . . to me he seemed to own the key to everything or almost everything worth having. But if ever I began to show the slightest idea of comradeship, he was immediately offended; and when once I suggested that I might help his private secretary to write some of his letters, he froze me into stone . . . Unable to accept the fact that he had never really been able to get close to his father, Winston, more than forty years after Lord Randolph's death, was still wistfully regretful . . . I know now that this would have been only a passing phase. Had he lived for another four or five years he could not have done without me. But there were no four or five years! Just as friendly relations were ripening into an Entente . . . he vanished for ever. . .

In the new-found spirit of camaraderie, Winston wrote to his father on 27th October congratulating him on a speech and on a win at the races . . . **Many congratulations on your Yarmouth speech and on "Molly Morgan". I hope you backed her well – I won two pounds myself.** He then went on to detail his proposed weekend leave arrangements . . . **If you will allow me I will go tomorrow (Friday) to sleep the night with Mr Little. Saturday morning I will come up to town and go to the Duchess Lily – who has asked me to spend Saturday and Sunday with her. I can thus see Mama and perhaps run down to Harrow in the afternoon . . . Thank you so much for sending two boxes of your best cigarettes. I keep them for after lessons and smoke commoner ones in the daytime . . .**

Lord Randolph took exception to Winston's plans. When he received his letter he wrote to the Duchess . . . *He comes back here on tomorrow. He wanted to go & stay with Dss Lily but I told him he had seen nothing of his mother & ought to devote himself to her. For some reason or other also I do not care about his being with the Duchess Lily . . . You never know what state she may be in . . .*

Cigarettes were one thing but cigars another. Winston reported to his father that Lady Randolph had . . . **written to me to tell me that you do not like my smoking cigars. I will not do so anymore, I am not fond enough of them in having any difficulty in leaving them off . . .** A week later Winston declared . . . **I will take your advice about the cigars – and I don't think I shall often smoke more than one or two a day – and very rarely that . . .** In the

event his prediction proved to be very wide of the mark. The letter continued . . . **I went on Sunday to see grandmama – who was staying with the Duchess Lily. I stayed there all day – as I had not seen grandmama for more than 3 months . . .** Winston, who liked Duchess Lily and was aware of his father's objections to her, had found a plausible excuse for his visit.

To his mother, Winston felt no need to dissemble . . . **Sunday I went to see the Duchess Lily and found Grandmamma there.** In the same letter he tells her he had seen Colonel Brabazon, an impoverished Irish landlord whose dashing character had more than compensated for his impecunious background. He had known Lord and Lady Randolph for many years and

Above: Colonel Brabazon

now commanded the 4th Hussars at Aldershot. Winston had not mentioned this encounter to Lord Randolph, who had pulled strings to get him into the 60th Rifles, presumably as he knew it would irritate his father. To Lady Randolph he felt safe in saying . . . **How I wish I was going into his regiment.** The writing was on the wall.

The financial straits in which Lord and Lady Randolph found themselves created a painful situation in the shared house in Grosvenor Square. Winston, unaware of the true state of his parents' finances (which would certainly not have been a subject for discussion), sprang to the support of Mrs Everest who, in effect if not in manner, was being dismissed. He wrote from Sandhurst on 29th October . . . **I have felt very uncomfortable since I got here about Everest . . . I feel I ought in common decency write to you at length on the subject.**

In the first place if I allowed Everest to be cut adrift without protest in the manner which is proposed I should be extremely ungrateful . . . because she is in my mind associated more than anything else with *home* **. . .**

Look too at the manner in which it would be done. She is sent away – nominally for a holiday because there is no room at Grosvenor Square for her. Then her board wages are refused her – quite an unusual thing. Finally she is to be given her *congé* **by letter – without having properly made up her mind where to go or what to do.**

. . . It is in your power to explain to the Duchess that she cannot be sent away until she has got a good place.

She has for 3 months been boarding herself out of her own money and I have no doubt is not at all well off . . . If you can arrange with the Duchess & persuade her to let Everest stay until after Christmas – I should feel extremely relieved. If you can't, I will write and explain things to Papa . . .

Winston, who was usually at pains to please Lord Randolph, was clearly prepared for a confrontation in defence of Mrs Everest. His mother was no help on this occasion and his stand was to little avail. Lady Randolph, an American brought up in Paris, had never established the special relationship peculiar to British employers and their long-serving nannies, a combination of intimacy and mutual respect. Mrs Everest kept up a correspondence with Winston and Jack but spent much of the two years which remained to her with a previous employer, Mrs Philips, wife of the Archdeacon of Barrow-in-Furness.

For some years there had been an estrangement between Lord Randolph and his brother Lord Blandford who, upon becoming the eighth Duke, virtually closed the doors of Blenheim to Lord Randolph and his family. Thus Winston was denied access to the happy playground of his childhood. The situation eased when Winston's cousin, Sunny, became the ninth Duke of Marlborough in November 1892. By Christmas Lady Blandford, the eighth Duke's first wife and Sunny's mother, had returned to Blenheim and invited Winston to stay.

On Christmas Day he wrote to his mother . . . **I am enjoying myself here very much – though there is plenty of divine service. Everyone is very kind and civil to me & Lady Blandford has really gone out of her way to make me comfortable. I suggested going on Tuesday but she would not hear of it & told me she expected me to stay until the following Monday. It would be very convenient if I could go direct from here to Hindlip as it is only an hour and a quarter – by train.**

. . . Altogether I am quite content at the prospect of staying here & am in no hurry to get back to town . . . For once he was in no hurry to take his leave in London.

After Christmas Winston, Lady Randolph and Jack were to spend a few days with Lord and Lady Hindlip in Worcestershire. Meanwhile, on Boxing Day, he hunted for the first time and, as he described in a letter on 30th December to his mother, went shooting with . . . **half a dozen keepers to drive one of the biggest covers. I had real sport and shot about 25 Rabbits and a dozen pheasants . . .** He continued . . . **I shall be extremely sorry to leave on Monday and nothing but the thought of the beautiful Polly Hacket consoles me . . .** Throughout his life Winston enjoyed being in the company of beautiful women, although for conversation he preferred men. And, susceptible though he was to the charms of the opposite sex, they were never allowed to divert him from his objectives.

Several days later Winston received the marks for his first examination at Sandhurst. He was placed eighth, having obtained 1,198 marks out of a possible 1,500. It was a creditable performance. His conduct was described as "Good but unpunctual".

Winston stayed on at Hindlip Hall after his mother had left. While still there he wrote to her, making clear that, despite his apparent acquiescence, he did not intend to pursue his military career in the infantry. Leaving nothing to chance, Winston explained his case fully, hoping, no doubt, that Lady Randolph would work on his father.

Hindlip Hall
11 January

My dearest Mamma,

I have written to Colonel Brabazon and have stated my various arguments in favour of cavalry regiment. I have asked him to say whether or no they are correct – when he writes to you – but in case he should not state this clearly I will put them down for you.

1. Promotions are much quicker in Cavalary [sic] than in Infantry. (60th Rifles slowest regiment in the army.)

2. Obtain your commission (3 or 4 months) in Cav much sooner than in Infantry.

3. 4th Hussars are going to India shortly . . . I should have 6 or 7 subalterns below me in a very short time.

4. Cavalry regiments are always given good stations in India and generally taken great care of by the Government – while Infantry have to take what they can get.

5. If you want to keep a horse you can do it much cheaper in the cavalry than in infantry – government will provide stabling – forage – and labour.

6. Sentimental advantages grouped under heading of
   a. uniform
   b. increased interest of a "life among horse" etc
   c. advantages of riding over walk
   d. advantages of joining a regiment whose officers you know. i.e. 4th Hussars.

The first 5 of these reasons I wrote to Col Brabazon the last I write to you.

There you are – now don't ever say I did not give you any reasons. There are 5 good solid arguments.

Now to other matters. I try hard to write large enough to please you but it looks unsightly especially when you like a great deal written on one page. However if you like it I will continue the practice.

What did the doctors say last night? Do send me a line sometime, Sunny is coming here on Monday – and I should like very much to stop until Wednesday. The ball being Thursday.

With best love and kisses I remain,
Ever your loving son
Winston

Winston had, during the Christmas holiday at Blenheim, formed a very favourable impression of his cousin Sunny with whom he had previously had very little contact. This was the beginning of a firm, lifelong friendship.

Winston, for all his intellectual maturity, was completely unsophisticated as far as girls were concerned. The New Year visit to Hindlip Hall was the beginning of his first known friendship with a woman. Lady Hindlip's niece, Molly (sometimes known as Polly) Hacket, and Winston became friends and met and corresponded on and off for more than a year. His tentative and clumsy approach and somewhat patronising and chauvinistic attitude towards the opposite sex are evident in various letters written at this time. He reported to Jack on 31st January . . . *Polly Hacket came for a walk this morning & we went and strolled Bond Street way . . .* On the same day his walking companion wrote to Winston:

Wednesday   *33 Hill Street*

My dear Winston,

Did you really mean to leave all those lovely sweets for me it was too too kind of you; if I had not been obliged to go and change we could have had a "stuff". The wedding was a great success and Nellie a wonder, so composed.

Alex's address is
    Mothercome
      Ivy Bridge
        S. Devon
I saw the Duke at Chesterfield Street. No chance of staying for the ball alas.

In great haste, hope we may meet again soon. Again many thanks for sugar plums.

Yrs v:sincerely
Molly Hacket

Molly's delight at the sugar plums must have been somewhat deflated by Winston's request for the address of another girl, Alex, the daughter of Major General Sir Arthur Ellis, Equerry to the Prince of Wales. On 13th February Molly wrote . . . *Many thanks for your letter. Quite proper . . . I was so sorry not to be at the dance, it must have been fun, did you dance with the 2nd Mrs H's niece? . . . How is dear Jack. When I am in London again & if you are too we will go down & see him . . .* Judging by her letters Molly was working herself up to be quite interested in Winston. On 4th March she began to worry that she might have a rival . . . *Do you often hear from Alex, she is going to London on Friday. I suppose you will go and see her, how you will talk. I wish*

I could join you, what fun! I shall be very jealous if you go very often to see her – but she is a great dear and so amusing . . . Shall you take Alex for a walk? . . . By the end of March Molly was a bit more confident . . . *I have been waiting for yr photograph which you promised and I want so much . . . when we arrive you will come and see me won't you? . . .* and then the anxious enquiry whether Winston had seen the girl whose address she had sent him six weeks earlier . . . *Do you often see Alex? . . . Don't forget the photograph . . .*

At the same time that Winston was being asked for his photograph by Molly Hacket, he was himself trying to obtain signed photographs of another object of his admiration. Mabel Love, a showgirl who appeared in a variety of productions including the Folies Bergère, wrote to Winston . . . *I am so sorry for not having returned the photos sooner but I have been very busy lately . . . I am afraid I don't know anything funny or amusing so I have just written my name. I shall look forward to seeing you when you come to town . . .*

Winston was evidently sufficiently proud of this acquaintance to report to his friend George Wilson who wrote . . . *How did you manage to meet Mabel Love, I rather envy you . . .*

The desultory friendship between Winston and Molly carried on and in June Winston reported to Jack that he . . . *had tea with Molly Hacket. I am going to bring her down to Harrow . . . altogether a very pleasant Sunday and not too expensive . . .* In July he wrote to Lady Randolph . . . *Yesterday Molly Hacket and I made our great expedition to Harrow – quite alone . . .* This was more significant than it may seem as these were the days when well-brought-up girls did not go out with young men unchaperoned. By October Winston was writing to his mother . . . *I have seen Miss Hacket a good deal lately . . .*

Winston was invited to spend the following Christmas at Hindlip with Molly's aunt but the invitation was over-taken by events beyond anyone's control. By the middle of the following year Winston received an invitation to

Above: Mabel Love

Above: Molly Hacket

Molly's wedding to Edward Wilson. This was the first of many friends that Winston would see wed before his own marriage to Clementine Hozier took place thirteen years and so many adventures later.

Mrs Everest, as solicitous as ever for the welfare of her "Boys", continued a brisk correspondence with them. She wrote at the end of January, anxious lest Jack's birthday should pass unnoticed . . . *I had a letter from dear Jackie he is so afraid you & everyone will not think of his little birthday 9th of next month. Do try & think of it dear & send him something & also remind Her Ladyship for He does not like to be forgotten poor Boy, he says no one thought of him last year but me. I have been busy making my room comfortable it is frightfully cold here. I hope you will keep your promise & come & see me on Sunday . . . I hope you will keep well dear – do you miss me a little bit . . . I have got my little room nice & comfortable now. I hope you will come & see me . . . Goodbye my Darling best love to you*

From your affecte old Woom
Please burn this do not leave my letters about.

There does not seem to be anything of sufficient importance in her letters to require their disposal. Perhaps Mrs Everest did not want Lady Randolph to realise that even though she had left Grosvenor Square she continued to provide the boys with a measure of security.

She was clearly living in straitened circumstances and might have expected to have been treated better. However, there was never a word of reproach from her. Rather she was concerned with the health and happiness of Winston and Jack. She wrote four more times during the following four weeks, worrying about Winston's health and the measurements of a cover she was making for a box . . . *Poor old boy I am so sorry you are troubled with tooth ache do get some spirits of camphor & rub some on your gums & also on your cheek frequently . . . I hope the Boils are dying away & that you are feeling better dear Boy . . . Well my darling what about your Box cover will you measure the box length & width & height & I will soon make it . . . mind you measure it correctly . . . I will enclose my yard measure . . . On a practical note . . . I was very much surprised to hear Mama had sent me a cheque. I have never recd either cheque or a letter from anyone at G.Square . . .* A few days later when Winston had made it his business to track down the elusive cheque . . . *I also duly recd your letter on Monday morning with cheque enclosed . . . It was very kind of you to see after it for me dear . . .* and on a more moralistic plane . . . *Be a good Gentleman upright honest just kind & altogether lovely. My sweet old darling how I do love you so be good for my sake.*

To add to the afflictions of boils and toothache, Winston had caught influenza in January while staying with the Duchess on leave in London. The illness interrupted his riding lessons which had been arranged with the riding master of the Life Guards, Captain Burt. On 31st January he wrote to his father, who was staying with Lady Wilton in Monte Carlo . . . *The Influenza has quite gone away . . . It was a great pity that it should come to interrupt my riding lessons just as I was hoping to steal a march on the other Cadets . . . I think I shall be able to arrange with Capt Burt to ride in the afternoon occasionally – as well as the mornings and so I may make up for the fortnight I was absent . . .*

I wonder if when you come back you would put my name down for a good club. You see in three years I shall be going out to India and – if I don't get in to some club soon it will not be much good to me.

. . . Please give my best love to Lady Wilton who wrote me such a kind letter . . .

Winston's recent lunch at Whites with his cousin Sunny had opened his eyes to the benefits to be derived from a London club. His reference to India "in three

---

138, PICCADILLY.

MENU DU SOUPER,

2 FEVRIER, 1894.

Huîtres au Citron.

Consommé chaude à la Printanière.
Cailles bardées aux feuilles de Vigne.

Coquilles de Crême de hômard.
Filets de Soles à la Belle Vue.
Chaud-froid de Mauviettes à la Jardinière.
Tomates à l'Algérienne.
Côtelettes à la Bohémienne
Sandwiches à la Chesterfield.
Poulets rôtis aux Cressons.
Jambon et Langue de Bœuf découpée.

Bananas à la Crême frappée.
Gelées aux Raisins.
Gelées à la Dauphine.
Poudings Nesselrode.
Crême au Chocolat.
Crême à la Vanille.

years" suggests that he was determined to join Colonel Brabazon and the 4th Hussars who were due to embark for India soon after Winston was due to join a regiment. Lord Randolph either missed or ignored the reference when he replied . . . *Well I do hope you will do better this quarter even than you did last . . . you must keep the standard up & keep raising. This is the critical time at Sandhurst . . . Pull yourself together & keep yourself well abreast & even ahead of those you are competing with. I rather advise you not to come up to London too often. Your mother & I can run down . . . It does not seem such an awful journey . . . take care of your health. Keep down the smoking, keep down the drink & go to bed as early as you can . . . Well I have written you a regular lecture but it is all sound. The better you do the more I shall be inclined to help you . . .* The manner in which Winston addressed his father was a source of irritation for Lord Randolph . . . *By the way I think you may substitute "Father" for "Papa"* . . . The Victorian father felt that his son was too old to use the more affectionate term but for Winston to whom he had been Papa for all of his twenty years it was not so simple.

Winston replied promptly beginning his letter **My dear Papa.** On the same day he wrote to Lady Randolph.

My dear Mamma,

I am much better to-day all round. The boils are healing up and I do not think that they will have to be lanced again. My tooth is still very troublesome but I think it will get better gradually . . .

I am sending you a list of the things I should like for my room. Please let me have what you can – as soon as possible as it is very uncomfortable at present . . .

Ever your loving son
Winston S. Churchill

PS I found such a kind letter from Papa (6 pages) waiting for me when I got back.   WSC

Winston had been put at the head of his riding class . . . *Horses were the greatest of my pleasures at Sandhurst . . . I enjoyed the riding-school thoroughly, and got on – and off – as well as most* . . . Lord Randolph, who earlier had questioned Winston's need even to hire a horse, was now taking a more benevolent view of his son's enthusiasm for riding, writing on 21st February . . . *I am glad to hear your riding has been so successful . . . I will give the 2gs fee for Captn Burt, 1 sov for the groom and a sov for the man who*

got your breakfast. If they object to you giving those sums to the 2 last men you can say I sent it specially on account of yr success at Sandhurst & the benefit you received from only a few & interrupted lessons . . . Winston was confident of his progress . . . **I was pretty well trained to sit and manage a horse** . . . and happy in his work . . . **No hour of work is lost that is spent in the saddle** . . .

Lord Randolph ended with more advice on study . . . *Why don't you read books on Saturday & Sunday. I will send you some* . . . Meanwhile Jack had complained to Winston that letters were *very scarce*. Winston replied by return of post . . . **I am sorry nobody has written to you – but Papa has been, I expect, very busy. I shall be coming down to Harrow next Saturday and will wire my train** . . . **PS Such a good letter you wrote me – & I am sorry to have so little to say.**

This was tactful as the day after commiserating with Jack he wrote to his father . . . **Thank you so much for writing to me – it is so good of you when you have so many things to do and think about** . . . Relations between Lord Randolph and Winston were improving.

The burgeoning relationship between father and son received a setback during Winston's second term at Sandhurst when two accidents in quick succession befell his watch. The gold half-hunter with the Churchill coat of arms with sixteen quarterings on the back in enamel had been a present from his father. Winston, fully aware of the trouble he would be in if the damage was discovered, immediately took the watch to be repaired. As luck would have it Lord Randolph had reason to visit the watchmaker, who had no qualms about customer confidentiality. Lord Randolph wrote angrily to Winston.

50 Grosvenor Square
21 April 1894

Dear Winston,
I have received your letter of yesterday's date & am glad to learn that you are getting on well in your work. But I heard something about you yesterday which annoyed & vexed me very much. I was at Mr Dent's about my watch, and he told me of the shameful way in which you had misused the very valuable watch which I gave you. He told me you had sent it to him some time ago, having with the utmost carelessness dropped it on a stone pavement & broken it badly. The repairs of it cost £3.17s which you will have to pay Mr Dent. He then told me he had again received the watch the other day and that you told him it had been dropped in the water . . . I would not believe you could be such a young stupid. It is clear you are not to be trusted with a valuable watch . . . You had better buy one of those cheap

watches for £2 . . . Jack has had the watch I gave him longer than you have had yours; the only expenses I have paid on his watch was 10/s for cleaning . . . in all qualities of steadiness taking care of his things & never doing stupid things Jack is vastly your superior.

Your vy much worried parent
Randolph S. Churchill

Lord Randolph wrote later the same day to Lady Randolph who was in Paris . . . *I was glad to get your letter & to learn that you were having such a good time* . . . *I have written a letter to Winston he won't forget* . . . *the old Mr Dent was quite concerned at one of best class of watches being treated in such a manner* . . . *Well I have told Winston that when the watch is put in order I shall not give it back again* . . . *I have advised him to buy one of those cheap £2 watches* . . . *You see I was very angry for I cannot understand anybody not taking the greatest care of a good watch, but also because he never told me a word about it. However as I said he won't forget my letter for some time & it will be a long time before I give him anything worth having. I wanted you to know this as he may tell a very different story* . . .

Lord Randolph's extreme reaction on learning about Winston's watch was no doubt conditioned by his illness. Lady Randolph would have had that in mind when she wrote to Winston on 22nd April.

Hotel Scribe
Sunday

Dearest Winston,

I am so sorry you have got into trouble over yr watch –
Papa wrote to me all about it . . . However he wrote very
kindly about you so you must not be too unhappy . . . Oh!
Winny what a harum scarum fellow you are! You really must
give up being so childish. I am sending you £2 with my love.
I shall scold you well when we meet.

Yr loving
Mother

She had credited Lord Randolph with sentiments far removed from those expressed in his letter and provided Winston with money for the cheap watch.

Meanwhile Winston was offering an explanation.

Sandhurst
21 April

My dear Father,

I have been very unfortunate about the watch – which I kept safely the whole time I was at James's – during our tour of Switzerland – and all last term. But about 6 weeks ago I broke it and within a fortnight of its being mended it is broken again. So really I have had it for over a year without an accident and then come 2 in a fortnight. Yet I have been no less careful of it during that fortnight than during the preceding year.

The first accident was not my fault at all. I had a leather case made for the watch – during the daytime to protect it and I was putting it into it when it was knocked out of my hand by a boy running past.

This time I am more to blame. I placed the watch (last Sunday) in my breast pocket – not having with uniform a waistcoat to put it in – and while walking along the Wish Stream I stooped to pick up a stick and it fell out of my pocket into the only deep place for miles.

The stream was only about 5 inches deep – but the watch fell into a pool nearly 6 feet deep.

I at once took off all my clothes and I dived for it but the bottom was so uneven and the water so cold I could not stay in longer than 10 minutes and had to give it up.

The next day I had the pool dredged – but without result. On Tuesday therefore I obtained permission from the Governor to do anything I could provided I paid for having it all put straight again.

I then borrowed 23 men from the Infantry Detachment – dug a new course for the stream – obtained the fire engine and pumped the pool dry and so recovered the watch. I tell you all this to show you that I appreciated fully the value of the watch and that I did not treat the accident in a casual way. The labour of the men cost me over £3.

I would rather you had not known about it. I would have paid for its mending and said nothing. But since you know about it – I feel I ought to tell you how it happened in order to show you that I really valued the watch and did my best to make sure of it.

I quite realise that I have failed to do so and I am very sorry that it should have happened. But it is not the case with all my things. Everything else you have ever given me is in as good repair as when you gave it first.

Opposite: The Wish Stream

Please don't judge me entirely on the strength of the watch. I am very sorry about it.

I am sorry to have written you such a long and stupid letter, but I do hope you will take it in some measure as an explanation.

With best love, I remain ever your loving son
Winston S. Churchill

The letter provides an interesting view of the young Winston in action. For a cadet he demonstrated quite extraordinary initiative in the measures he took to recover the watch. His action stuck in the mind of Captain Armstrong who at the time was a fellow cadet and who wrote to Winston twelve years later . . . *I saw a picture of you helping to put a fire out, it reminded me of the incident at the R.M.C. when you lost your watch & persuaded the whole of "E" Company to assist in pumping the pond dry . . .*

The letter also illustrates Winston's earnest desire to retain his father's affection and respect. Why else the abject apology for writing such a long and stupid letter when, in fact, it is a well-constructed explanation?

Winston was cheered by his mother's letter and he wrote back by return of post.

My dearest Mamma,

Thank you so much for your letter – which I have just received. Papa . . . seems to be very cross. I wrote back at once saying how sorry I was and explaining the whole affair & got a letter by return of post – last night. I think by his letter Papa is somewhat mollified. I hope so indeed. But how on earth could I help it. I had no waistcoat to put the watch in and so have had to wear it in the pocket of my tunic.

Papa writes, he is sending me a Waterbury – which is rather a come down.

I am very sorry it should have happened – as you can well believe – and sorrier still that Papa should have heard of it. But I feel quite clear in my own mind that I am not to blame except for having brought so good a watch back here – where there is everything in the way of its safety.

However Waterbury is as the regulations say "more suited to my position as a cadet" and there is not much time to lament, here now.

It is so dear of you to have written me a kind letter & for sending me the £2. You are the best and sweetest mamma in all the world. With lots of love & kisses,

I remain Ever your loving son
Winston S. Churchill

On the same day Winston wrote to his father . . . I know I have been very foolish and clumsy with the watch and fully deserve to have it taken away. I am very sorry to have been so stupid and careless – but I hope that you will not be cross with me any more about it – and that you will accept what I say as to being an isolated case of not taking care of things . . .

The £2 from Lady Randolph did not, after all, have to be spent on a watch. Within a week of his angry letter, Lord Randolph had sent Winston a Waterbury. He wrote on 1st May in a much more conciliatory tone:

Dear Winston,

You need not trouble any more about the watch. It is quite clear that the rough work of Sandhurst is not suitable for a watch made by Dent . . . If you would like to come up on the 5th of May I am afraid you won't find me at dinner for I dine at the Royal Academy dinner, but your mother will be here & you might do a play.

Ever your affte father
Randolph S.C.

Jack did not want to miss out on the family drama. He wrote from Harrow on 2nd May . . . *Why hav'ent I heared all these goings on before, how silly to have broken the watch!!!! Mama said Papa was furious, she came down here yesterday . . . Do write! and let me know how the watch happened. . . .*

Winston's reply shows that for him the watch saga was over . . . As to the watch: it's a long story . . . Meanwhile I have an excellent Waterbury which keeps far better time than the gold one . . .

This air of bravado had to be maintained for much longer than Winston might have reasonably expected. The watch, which had narrowly missed being pawned a few months earlier, was never restored to him. After Lord Randolph's death it passed to Jack who wore it all his life, thus presenting Winston with a constant reminder of his father's humiliating action. The watch which had been through so much is no longer in the family. On Jack's death it passed to his eldest son, John, from whom it was stolen.

For a young man of nineteen and a half Winston was not given much freedom of movement. His actions were to a large extent governed by what he could afford. Lord Randolph did not want his son to spend his free time in London. London cost money, of which Winston never had enough. His financial situation was a reflection of that of his parents. The Churchills, in comparison to their friends, led a hand-to-mouth existence, staying with Duchess Fanny in Grosvenor Square, while

Winston existed on a drip-feed economy which did nothing to teach him how to balance his own budget.

The restrictions on visits to London did not prevent Winston finding diversions elsewhere. At the end of April Lady Randolph wrote . . . *A bird whispered to me that you did not sleep in yr own bed last night. Write to me all about it. I am not sure if Papa wld approve . . .* It is not clear if Lady Randolph knew where Winston had been, or whether it would have been his absence or his actual whereabouts which would have met with his father's disapproval. Winston replied to Lady Randolph with a disingenuous interpretation of Lord Randolph's instructions to avoid London. By staying in Aldershot with the 4th Hussars, albeit with the Cavalry of which his father disapproved, he was avoiding London . . . **I should not think that Papa would object to my having stayed with Col Brab at Aldershot. He distinctly wrote to me that he did not want me to come up to London much. I wrote yesterday and told him all about it . . . I had great fun at Aldershot – the regiment is awfully smart – I think they did not always have a good name – but Col Brab did not take long in knocking them into shape . . . How I wish I was going into the 4th instead of those old Rifles. It would not cost a penny more & the regiment goes**

to India in 3 years which is just right for me. I hate the Infantry – in which physical weakness will render me nearly useless on service & the only thing I am showing an aptitude for athletically – riding – will be no good to me . . . it is not much good writing down these cogent arguments – but if I pass high at the end of term I will tackle Papa on the subject . . .

Lord Randolph raised no objection to Winston's visit to the 4th Hussars. He disposed of the subject in a single sentence in his next letter . . . *I daresay you had a pleasant Sunday with Colonel Brabazon . . .* As yet he was unaware of Winston's determination to join the cavalry and judged the high life of London as a greater threat to his vision of Winston's military career.

A colourful event in the Sandhurst calendar was the annual parade after the half-mile donkey race. This was an open day at the college when the cadets wore fancy-dress and invited guests. Winston, not unreasonably but perhaps optimistically, hoped that his mother would visit him. In a manner reminiscent of his pleading letters from Harrow and with the same lack of success Winston wrote on 9th May . . . I *do* hope you will come down on Friday. I have got a luncheon ticket in expectation and I am sure you

The Donkey Race.

will be much amused . . . please come & give great pleasure to Your ever loving son . . . Do get me a dress . . . Something amusing . . . and the next day . . . So sorry and disappointed to find you can't come down. Had hoped you would be able to spare a day . . . I am sure you would not be bored . . . If you find that it is impossible to come Please try and get me a costume and send it by the *guard* of the train at 11.45. I will meet it. Try and get a *gorilla* or something amusing. I do hope you will do so as I have paid 10/– for the entrance and if no costume then I can't ride . . . Neither his efforts to entice her by the attractions on offer nor his wistful remarks designed to make her feel guilty succeeded but she did send him a clown costume and on 13th May he wrote . . . Thank you so much for sending me the dress which I wore & which did very well . . . It was perhaps just as well that you did not come down after all – for it poured with rain the whole day and I am sure you would have been very bored . . .

Winston was exaggerating when he wrote that his physical weakness would handicap him in the Infantry. His subsequent daring exploits while on active service during the Boer War demonstrated his stamina. Nevertheless his physique was well below average at Sandhurst and his constitution far from robust. On arrival at the Academy he had been listed among those cadets whose chest measurement had to increase before they could be commissioned.

His first two terms were marred by boils, influenza and for much of the second term with a particularly bad toothache. In May he wrote to Lord Randolph saying that he was . . . **troubled with the most abominable headaches . . . On Friday they made me come into hospital** . . . A lesser young man would have become dispirited with such a catalogue of ills but Winston's stride never faltered. From hospital, despite his headache, he wrote to his father that he was . . . **reading up a very good work . . . on Tactics & making typewritten notes . . . I hope to be out on**

Above and opposite: The Donkey Race with Winston in clown costume

Sunday . . . He was, characteristically, too optimistic and it was not until the following Sunday that he was released.

He had meanwhile written to Lady Randolph thanking her for a cheque . . . **which was very welcome – though I should have preferred a more gracious letter** . . . She had reminded him that . . . *this makes £6 I have given you the last month* . . . and that Lord Randolph . . . *wld be very X if he knew I gave you money* . . . Winston showed his appreciation for the extra funds by grandly explaining . . . **Everything seemed very crude here but I judiciously distributed a few half crowns and am consequently looked after "en prince"** . . . He continued after remarking on the state of his health . . . **I think a few days quiet & rest & peaceful treatment will elevate my soul & strengthen my broken spirit** . . . Winston would have been wise to have ended his letter there but he injudiciously went on . . . **Do write me a letter and tell me some other news, than the fact I have for some time recognised V.I.Z. that I spend too much money** . . .

Lady Randolph, although informal in her dealings with her son, was not amused by this brash letter. She wrote . . . *My only way of showing my displeasure is by silence* . . . Winston closed the incident by replying . . . **can't possibly imagine what I said to anger you** . . .

Having time on his hands, Winston continued to write to his nearest and dearest giving them details of his latest indisposition. Mrs Everest, who could always be counted upon for a sympathetic reaction, hastened to give him the benefit of her own particular brand of medical advice.

My Darling,

I recd both your letters & am very sorry to hear you are not feeling well. What can it be – I am afraid you are not careful about your eating. Have you tried some of Eno's fruit salt – it would do you a lot of good – take a teaspoonful every morning with the juice of a lemon & a bit of sugar it will do your liver good you try it. You have not been bathing in the lake yet I hope . . . Have you seen the Doctor don't neglect yourself if you don't feel well darling a stitch in time saves 99 & let me hear how you are as I shall feel anxious now you have told me you are not well . . . I am longing to see my two dearest Boys again. I hope my dear Winny is not being led away & getting into dissipated habits . . .

From your Affecte old
Woom

While Lady Randolph maintained her silence to punish Winston for his impertinent letter on 28th May, Lord Randolph gave his opinion . . . *Sick head-* aches sound much like biliousness . . . have care in your diet & in your manner of eating. Eating fast as you do, is a fertile source of indigestion biliousness & heated blood producing boils . . . till you learn to chew your food properly, as I do . . . you will always be subject to derangements of the digestive organ . . . He then returned to the manner in which Winston addressed him, which was still a source of irritation . . . You oscillate between "Dear Father" and "Dear Papa". I think you had better stick to the former . . . Usually keen to please his father this was a lesson Winston either would not or could not learn, for on 19th June Lord Randolph again complained . . . How stupid you are you do not stick to "my dear father" & relapse into "my dear Papa". This is idiotic . . . Idiotic indeed but this had become an important issue to the older man.

*Below and opposite: Always keen to experiment, Winston
acquired a new toy*

Royal Military College,

Sandhurst,

June 5..1894.

My dear Mamma,

I hope you have no old fashioned prejudices against the

Typewriter.   I sent you a telegrap to day to ask if Papa had

got the letter that I wrote ti him last night.   i was siezed

with awild desire to go and see the Deruy.   The other cadets are

getting up a special and I culd without missing any work get to Epsom

in good time to see the Race.   So I wrote to Papa, as I did not

want to go incognito and have to pay all my own expensesetc. also ½

thought that he might not approve of my going without asking.

If you see him please make a combined assault with me.   Send me

a wire early as I should have to start at one.   I hope to come

up next Saturday and shall see you should you not see me tomorrow.

What a great success the Bradford meeting was.

Ever your loving son,

Winston J Churchill

Royal Military College,

June 7th. 1894.

My dear Father,

Thank you so much for your telegram. I had hoped that my letter would have reached you in time, but it was forwarded from London and I think got delayed there. I did not like to send a telegram as I thought the letter was rather a forlorn hope and that a wire would have to be very long to have been explicit. I wish indeed that I had. What a capital Horse. I suppose you backed him even though you had to give the odds. If your Epsom Meeting is half as successful as your Bradford meeting you ought to have a very good week. Next Saturday I should like to come up to town very much, if you don't mind. Every thing is going on very well especially the riding at which I am making much progress. The Examination at the end of the term is going to be set by the Headquarter Examiners, instead of the old fossils here so I hope to benefit by the extra work I have done in Hamley Mayne, & Prince Kraft, . Will you be going to Ascot? That is the great event of the year here. We can get over all three days but not always in time for the Gst race. You see that it is only 4 miles. With best love and wishing you very good luck and a pleasant meeting,

Ever your Loving son,

Winston S. Churchill

Lord Randolph, who meticulously replied to every point raised in the letters he received, wrote at length to Winston on 24th June giving him one item of good news . . . *I will see about the Club* . . . There then followed a detailed criticism of a letter he had received from Winston . . . *You write stupidly on what you call "the subject of finance"* . . . After dissecting the letter sentence by sentence he then made the usual comparison between the brothers . . . *Jack would have cut off his hand rather than write such a free-spoken letter to his father* . . . Lord Randolph then concluded crushingly . . . *This is a letter which I shall not keep but return it to you that you may from time to time review its pedantic & overgrown schoolboy style. Perhaps it is due to that stupid typewriter which I think an objectionable machine calculated to spoil your handwriting* . . . And then the parting shot . . . *if you are going to write letters to me when I am travelling, typewritten & so ridiculously expressed I would rather not receive them* . . .

Lord Randolph's criticism of his son's style of writing was quite unwarranted. Although Winston's letters were usually dashed off in a hurry, to convey information or more often requests, his writing, when he took care, was already developing the distinctive style and vocabulary for which he later became so famous.

Just as Winston seemed to be on the point of establishing a rapport, however fragile, with his father, Lord Randolph's health took a turn for the worse.

Lord Randolph was the only surviving son of the seventh Duke of Marlborough's eleven children. There were six daughters who lived to an average age of sixty-four. The five sons lived to an average age of twenty. The oldest, the eighth Duke, died at forty-eight and the youngest in his first year.

Winston's cousin and new-found friend, Sunny, had succeeded as the ninth Duke in 1892. For three years the only direct heirs to the dukedom were the ailing Lord Randolph and his two sons, both of whom were lucky to have survived their infancy and who were by no means robust. Winston had suffered a catalogue of illnesses and Jack had been born a blue baby with a defective right eye and a twisted main artery to the heart. It was as though there was a conspiracy to kill off the male Churchills.

No one will ever be sure of the true cause of Lord Randolph's death. The only certainty is that for some

time he had been suffering from an affliction of the brain which had affected his temperament, behaviour and powers of reason before resulting in coma and death.

Twenty-six years later Winston's enemies in the Conservative Party, in order to keep him from office, dubbed him the alcoholic son of a syphilitic father. Recent medical research, based on a reassessment of all the available facts, together with the symptoms he described in letters to his mother, indicates that Lord Randolph's death was the result of a deep-seated tumour of the brain.

Lord and Lady Randolph set off at the end of June on a voyage around the world . . . I was making a road map on Chobham Common in June 1894, when a cyclist messenger brought me the college adjutant's orders to proceed at once to London. My father was setting out the next day on a journey around the world. An ordinary application to the college authorities for my being granted special leave of absence had been refused as a matter of routine . . . Lord Randolph, normally most anxious that Winston should adhere to the rules, believed in bending them when it suited him . . . He had telegraphed to the Secretary of State for War Sir Henry Campbell-Bannerman, "My last day in England" . . . and no time had been lost in setting me on my way to London. . . .

Lord Randolph's doctors had prescribed rest for their patient who, seemingly oblivious of his mental condition, refused to accept this advice. As an alternative, travel was decided upon as the likeliest means of alleviating the situation. Had he remained at home he would have continued to distress his family and friends by his embarrassing public appearances both in the House of Commons and around the country. Because of the seriousness of Lord Randolph's illness, the Churchills were accompanied by the son of Lady Randolph's gynaecologist, Dr George Keith, who undertook to send weekly reports to Dr Roose in London.

. . . We drove to the station the next morning – my mother, my brother and I. In spite of the great beard which he had grown during his South African journey four years before, his face looked terribly haggard and worn with mental pain. He patted me on the knee in a gesture which however simple was perfectly informing.

There followed his long journey round the world. I never saw him again except as a swiftly-fading shadow.

Left: Winston and fellow cadets

Their parents gone, Winston and Jack were left under the guardianship of their grandmother, Duchess Fanny. Letters crossed exchanging news from all quarters. On 19th July the Duchess reported from Grosvenor Square . . . *You will be glad to hear the Boys are well. Jack is pursuing his quiet course at Harrow. Winston is here & on the strength of your and R's popularity is invited abt as much and perhaps more than you could wish. But its a great thing to keep him in good society . . . he has just asked my Leave to go to Sandown . . . This I have given him on his giving me his word of Honour he will not be induced to bet. It is difficult to refuse him anything . . . He is affectionate and pleasant but you know he is mercurial and plausible . . . he is very well and happy . . . but I fear he is thoughtless about money and I am always lecturing about economy but I fear with little success! . . . And eight days later . . . there is nobody but me to keep him in order and I am obliged to insist on punctuality and making him report himself once or twice a day . . . he is not like Jack & requires a firm hand . . .*

Once again the two boys were to spend their summer holiday travelling in Europe with Mr Little. On 22nd July the Churchills were at Bar Harbour in Maine and about to leave for Vancouver. Winston wrote to his mother . . . I am going to lunch with Little tomorrow . . . We have arranged our trip. It will be modified as we go by the funds and by the time we have – but it is roughly this. London – Brussels – Lucerne – Interlaken – Chamonix – Zermatt – Through the Furka pass – Goeschenen – Milan – Venice (if not too hot) – Innsbruck – Salzburg – Vienna. At Vienna I leave and return by the Orient Express to Sandhurst. Jack and Little will go back by easy stages – via Paris.

I have written Papa a long letter on the subject of Cavalry. I do so hope he will not be angry – or take it as "freespoken" or stupid. I only wrote what I thought he ought to know – namely how keen I was to go into the Cavalry and how I could not look forward with great eagerness to going with even the best Infantry regiment in the world . . .

On 3rd August he wrote from Brussels making sure that his mother knew that he missed her and that he was not in perfect harmony with the Duchess Fanny . . . We feel happy – but it is a horrid bore & worse not to have my own love to talk to. The duchess was getting very "difficile" when we left and it was perhaps just as well we came off here . . . I have annexed a beautiful photo of you with the star in your hair . . . Jack and I think of you every day . . .

The letter to Lord Randolph drew an uncompromising reply.

Hotel de Monte
California
21 August 1894

My dear Winston,

I do not enter into your lengthy letter of 22nd in which you enlarge on your preference for the Cavalry over the 60th Rifles. I could never sanction such a change. Your name was put down by myself on the Duke of Cambridge's list for one or other of the battalions of that Regiment. The Duke of Cambridge would be extremely angry with you if you were to make any application for such a change; His Royal Highness would consult me and I should oppose it strongly. So you had better put that out of your head altogether at any rate during my lifetime during which you will be dependent on me. So much for that subject.

Your other letters numbering five in all have been very charming & agreeable to receive & read . . . [Then followed a long and chatty letter ending] . . . *Love to Jack and remember me to Mr Little warmly.*

Your affectionate father
Randolph S. Churchill

During his third and final term at Sandhurst, Winston's writing was first published in a national newspaper and he made his first public speech. His début on the stage of public affairs arose because . . . my indignation was excited by the Purity Campaign of Mrs Ormiston Chant . . . an active movement to purge our music-halls. Her attention was particularly directed to the promenade of the Empire Theatre . . . where young people of both sexes . . . refreshed themselves with alcoholic liquors . . . Mrs Ormiston Chant and her friends . . . endeavoured to procure the closing of the Promenade and above all the bars which abutted on it. The issue was keenly debated among the Sandhurst cadets who frequented the promenade at weekends . . . We thought Mrs Ormiston Chant's movement entirely uncalled for and contrary to the best traditions of British freedom . . .

The *Westminster Gazette* of 18th October carried, above the initials WLSC, Winston's letter . . . The improvement in the standard of public decency is due rather to improved social conditions and

Above: Lord and Lady Randolph in San Francisco

*Above: Group photograph with Winston 3rd from right in
second row from top*

to the spread of education than to the prowling of the prudes . . . the only method of reforming human nature and of obtaining a higher standard of morality is by educating the mind of the individual and improving the social conditions under which he lives . . . It is slow but it is sure . . . Well meaning but misguided people, of which Mrs Ormiston Chant is a fair specimen, have prevailed upon Government to disclaim responsibility which it was their bounden duty to accept . . .

If our impetuous reformers could be persuaded to wait, and to take a broader and perhaps a more charitable view of social problems, they would better serve the cause they have at heart. But these "old women in a hurry" will not have patience, but are trying to improve things by repressive measures – a dangerous method, usually leading to reaction.

Winston's campaigning spirit did not stop at writing to the newspapers. Having read in the *Daily Telegraph* that there was to be a meeting in London of "the Entertainments Protection League", an organisation founded with the express purpose . . . to resist and counter the intolerance of Mrs Chant and her backers . . . I immediately volunteered my services . . . In due course I received an answer on impressively-headed notepaper . . . inviting my attendance at the first meeting of the Executive Committee . . . I occupied the three days' interval in composing a speech which I thought I might be called upon to deliver . . .

A first public speech is an ordeal for anyone but for Winston there was an added problem. It was around this time that he consulted Sir Felix Semon, an eminent throat specialist, with the request: "Cure the impediment in my speech, please. I'm going into the army first. But as a minister later, I can't be haunted by the idea that I must avoid every word beginning with an s." Before he had even got his commission in the Army he was already planning to enter the world of politics. Semon found no physical defect and prescribed "practice and perseverance" to cure the disability. When Winston was determined, he put all his energy into the project in hand. He spent many hours trying to get his tongue around sentences featuring the tiresome letter "s". He was to be heard walking up and down pronouncing "The Spanish ships I cannot see for they are not in sight". He did not succeed. The most famous speeches of all time were punctuated by Winston's problem with the letter "s". . .

. . . As I had never attempted to speak in public before, it was a serious undertaking. I wrote and re-wrote my speech three or four times over, and committed it in all its perfection to my memory . . . I awaited eagerly and at the same time nervously the momentous occasion . . . I drove in a hansom cab from Waterloo to Leicester Square . . . Winston had led a protected life . . . I was surprised and a little disconcerted at the dingy and even squalid appearance of these back streets and . . . the hotel when my cab eventually drew up . . . there I met face to face the Founder of the new body. He was alone. I was upset; but concealing my depression under the fast-vanishing rays of hope, I asked, "When do we go up to the meeting?" He too seemed embarrassed. ". . . there's only you and me," he added, "It's very difficult to get people to do anything in England now. They take everything lying down. I do not know what's happened to the country; they seem to have no spirit left."

. . . I bade him a restrained but decisive farewell, and walked out into the street with a magnificent oration seething within my bosom and only half a crown in my pocket . . . It was then that Winston encountered a side of life that he had hitherto avoided . . . I did what I had never done before or since. I had now reached the Strand. I saw the three golden balls hanging over Mr Attenborough's well-known shop . . . Some particulars were filled up in a book. I received one of those tickets which hitherto I had only heard of in music-hall songs . . . and sallied forth . . .

Most sons would have kept quiet about the visit to the pawnbroker, not Winston. He lost no time in using the episode to reinforce his request to his mother for money. On 19th September he wrote . . . the sovs & the 2 sovs & the 3 pounds used to make a great difference & now they have ceased altogether . . . I have had to pawn several of the things I used least . . . I am not in any way *seriously involved* but only extremely hard up . . . to Jack he wrote . . . I raised a tenner on a lot of old rubbish that I never want to see again . . .

Mrs Ormiston Chant and her "prowling prudes" succeeded in persuading the authorities to separate the promenade from the offending bars with canvas screens. These were demolished by an angry crowd and . . . the bars were once more united with the promenade to which they had ministered so long . . . In these somewhat unvirginal surroundings I now made my maiden speech. Mounting on the debris and indeed partially emerging from it, I addressed the tumultuous crowd. No accurate report of my words has been preserved. They did not, however, fall unheeded . . . I finished up by saying "You have seen us tear down these barricades to-night; see that you pull down those who are responsible at the coming election." These words were received with rapturous applause . . .

To Jack, Winston wrote proudly on 7th November . . . Did you see the papers about the riot at the Empire last Saturday. It was I who led the rioters – and made a speech to the crowd . . . In spite of his satisfaction at the success of his crusade Winston did have reservations . . . This episode made a considerable stir . . . I was for some time apprehensive lest undue attention should be focussed on my share in the proceedings . . . my father's name was still electric . . . They sometimes have a nasty trick of singling out individuals and "making examples". Although always prepared for martyrdom, I preferred that it should be postponed . . . This battle was not to go down as one of Winston's victories . . . The Progressives, as they called themselves, triumphed. The barricades were rebuilt in brick and plaster, and all our efforts went for nothing . . .

Lady Randolph had concealed from her sons the serious nature of their father's condition. The exchange of letters continued unabated as the Churchills progressed on their painful journey. During the six months that they were travelling they received more than thirty letters from Winston. For the first few months he wrote long and chatty letters giving them all manner of news but with little more than conventional enquiries after his father's health. But by 21st October he had begun to realise that all was not well . . . We are very much disturbed by Dr Keith's last letter which gives a very unsatisfactory report about Papa. I hope however that there is still an improvement and no cause for immediate worry . . .

On 29th October he wrote another long letter, this time to Lord Randolph . . . Grandmamma writes to me regularly about you so I am kept well informed . . . he continued with an account of happenings at Sandhurst, some political news, social activities and a mention of the "prudes'" victory over the Empire. He ended . . . Now my dearest father . . . I can't tell you how I long to hear of your improvement an how delighted I should be to see you again well and strong.

Hoping above all things that you are better.

I remain, Ever your loving and affectionate son
Winston S. Churchill

By 2nd November Winston was convinced that all was not as it had seemed. He wrote to Lady Randolph . . . I persuaded Dr Roose to tell exactly how Papa

was . . . You see I only hear through Grandmamma Jerome who does not take a very sanguine view of things – or through the Duchess who is at one extreme one minute and at the other the next . . . I need not tell you how anxious I am. I had never realised how ill Papa had been and never until now believed that there was anything serious the matter . . . then showing surprising maturity and sensitivity . . . Now about yourself. Darling Mummy I so hope that you are keeping well and that the fatigues of travelling as well as the anxiety you must feel about Papa – are not telling on you . . . and still showing concern for others . . . write nothing but good to the Duchess . . . She lives, thinks, and cares for nothing else in the world but to see Papa again . . .

In his letter to Lord Randolph of 8th November, Winston showed none of the anxiety he was feeling. Someone had asked after Lord Randolph and Winston wrote . . . I was able to give him a good report . . . I suppose this letter will catch you somewhere in India . . . I hope (to quote one of your own speeches) that all your worries will be "lulled by the languor of the land of the lotus" . . . Winston's apt quotation was culled from a speech by Lord Randolph in the House nine years earlier when he had been attacking the policies of Lord Ripon, Viceroy of India.

When she wrote to Winston from Singapore on 6th November, Lady Randolph was still unaware that he had discovered how serious was his father's illness and her letter gave nothing away. However, facing the imminent loss of her husband, the mask slipped as she worried about her eldest son . . . *don't be foolish about the riding – if anything should happen to you . . .*

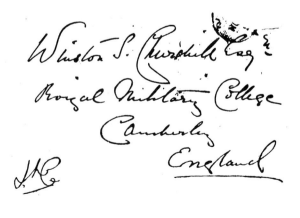

"Gov: Ct —"

GOVERNMENT HOUSE,
SINGAPORE.

Dearest Winston

The Govt: bag went this afternoon & the ordinary mail is closed — but the Colonial Sec. is leaving tonight for England, & I am sending this hasty line by him — a P.S. to my letter — You

[3] are to look after him? — I send you a cheque for £12. a present for yr birthday — don't tell anyone. Don't think it too much of an amusement — how about yr German?? Bless you darling — Thank Jack for me for his

ought to reach [2nd] by the X of Dec: An unexpected mail has come in — just caught me before our departure tomorrow — & yrs of the 15th & 19th & also one from Jack has come — Darling boy don't be foolish about the ending — if anything happened to you who [4] letter — Send my love to Aunt Clara — & tell her I will write without fail from B ch — I'm been too low to write — She will understand — In haste

Yr loving

Mother

J L C

Put a penny stamp & round than marked — & push yr initials across

To her sister Clara, Lady Randolph opened her heart as she sailed between Rangoon and Madras . . . *I cant tell you how I pine for a little society. It is so hard to get away from one's thoughts when one is always alone. And yet the worst of it is I dread the chance even of seeing people for his sake. He is quite unfit for society . . . at Govt House Singapore he was very bad for two days and it was dreadful being with strangers . . . I want if possible to get him home or at least near home . . . Of course he does not realize there is anything the matter with him as he feels well physically . . . cannot go into all the details of his illness but you cannot imagine anything more distracting & desperate than to watch it & see him as he is & to think of him as he was . . .*

Her morale was understandably low when she considered her own future . . . *I had a telegram from Charles [Count Kinsky] at Rangoon telling me of his engagement. I HATE IT. I shall return without a friend in the world & too old to make any more now . . .*

On 24th November it was decided to bring Lord Randolph home. On receiving the news Winston wrote to his mother.

> 50 Grosvenor Square
> 25 November

My darling Mama,

I was at Dr Roose's on Saturday & he showed me the telegram from Madras that had just arrived. I cannot tell you how shocked and unhappy I am – and how sad this heavy news makes me feel. I do not know – how far distant the end of poor dear Papa's illness may be – but I am determined that I will come out and see him again.

There is not much to write. You understand how I feel about him – and I do not care to write to you at such a time on commonplaces.

It must be awful for you – but it is almost as bad for me. You at least are there – on the spot & near him.

This is what you must try and do. Bring him back – at least as far as Egypt & if possible to the Riviera and I and Jack will come and join you there. Darling dearest Mummy keep your pluck & strength up. Don't allow yourself to think. Write to me exactly how he is. God bless you & help us all.

> Your loving son
> Winston

Write me an answer to this letter by return mail. Please.

To Jack, who at fourteen had been shielded from the serious implications of Lord Randolph's condition, Winston wrote more optimistically.

> Sandhurst
> 29 November

My darling Jack,

Papa & Mama are coming home and will be at Monte Carlo by the End of December – so we shall be able to go out there and see them. The doctors think that if he keeps perfectly quiet he may yet get well – though he will never be able to go into Politics again. Keep your spirits up & write to

> Your loving brother
> Winston

What was probably Winston's last letter to Lord Randolph described the final riding examination at Sandhurst. Had he been in a position to appreciate the letter, Lord Randolph would have been very pleased with his son's achievement.

Above: Jack

Sandhurst
9th December

My dearest Father,

You cannot think how delighted we all are to hear of your return for Christmas to Europe. It is splendid to be able to write to you and feel that this letter will reach you in only a few short days – instead of months.

The Riding Examination took place on Friday. First of all – all the cadets were examined who pass out this term – 127 in all. Then 15 were picked to compete together for the prize. I was one of those and in the afternoon we all rode – the General, Col Gough of the Greys and Capt Byng 10th Hussars, Judges – with dozens of officers and many more cadets as spectators. This riding for the prize is considered a great honour and the cadets take a great interest in it.

Well we rode – jumped with & without stirrups & without reins – hands behind back and various other tricks. Then 5 were weeded out leaving only ten of us. Then we went in the field & rode over the numerous fences several times. 6 more were weeded out leaving only 4 in. I was wild with excitement and rode I think better than I have ever done before but failed to win the prize by 1 mark being second with 199 out of 200 marks.

I am awfully pleased with the result, which in a place where everyone rides means a great deal, as I shall have to ride before the Duke and also as it makes it very easy to pick regts when the Colonels know you can ride. I hope you will be pleased.

The examinations begin tomorrow and I must have a last look round my Tactics. The competition is very keen and I am working hard. The result will not be known until January towards the end. I trust it may be satisfactory and that I shall find I have passed successfully out of Sandhurst.

As soon as I know the result and know that I have finished with the R.M.C. I will write to you if you are not home and you can then make arrangements for me.

I hope Mamma is well – I am writing to her. Jack and I long to see you both.

With best love, Ever your loving son
Winston S. Churchill

PS
I hope you will be pleased with the riding.

On the same day Winston wrote to his mother.

Sandhurst
9 December

My darling Mamma,

I am so glad to hear of your return. Write to me and let me know what you think and everything. I have written to Papa about riding prize – he will be pleased. Your dear letter with cheque arrived exactly on my birthday, as it chanced. The exams are to-morrow and I must work at them so this is but a hurried line.

I shall not know whether I have passed out of Sandhurst or not until end of January – so you can point out to Papa that it would be impossible for me to go to Germany until after that date. That will settle things for the present.

I do not wish to make difficulties or add to your labours my darling mummy – but I dont intend for one instant to exile myself in Germany with papa as ill as he is. As soon as I know about the exams I shall go at once to stay with you and him and will of course come sooner if you can arrange it.

Write soon.

With best love and kisses
My darling dearest Mummy
I remain, Ever your loving son
Winston

It had previously been suggested that Winston should go to Germany, to which he had replied that if he passed out of Sandhurst . . . **high – with honours – as is possible, I might be allowed to have some more fitting reward than the opportunity of mastering the German language.** Subsequently, on 17th December he offered an alternative . . . **If I were to go into the Cavalry I should get my commission in about 2 months to 2½ months instead of 6 or 7 months wait for Rifles. So that would obviate necessity of going to Germany . . .**

For Winston to have his life put on hold at this moment must have been extremely difficult. However much he loved his father and was distressed by his illness, there were decisions that could not wait. The one step that Winston wanted to take was to transfer from the Infantry to the Cavalry. This was the subject above all on which Lord Randolph had been obdurate – and therefore the one decision which could not in all decency be reversed while he lay on his deathbed. Having made his point, Winston continued . . . **Although I intend to be most submissive – I am firmly determined not to exile myself in Germany while my father is ill . . .**

There was no reaction from Lord Randolph, and Lady Randolph was preoccupied by the problem of getting her increasingly ailing husband back to England.

On Christmas Eve Lord and Lady Randolph reached London where they returned to stay with the Duchess in Grosvenor Square. During the next month Lord Randolph occasionally rallied. Lady Randolph's sister Clara wrote to her younger sister Leonie that he had asked Winston about his Sandhurst results and had recognised and smiled at Jack. But these were mere flickers of consciousness and finally Winston was summoned for the last time . . . **My father died on January 24 in the early morning . . . His end was quite painless . . .**

When seventy years later the ninety-year-old Winston himself lay dying, the wheels of bureaucracy were poised to put into action arrangements long since made for his final journey. A pall of gloom hung over London while Winston lingered on to fulfil his own prediction that he would die on the anniversary of Lord Randolph's death.

So it was that early in the morning on 24th January 1965, seventy years later to the day, surrounded by his wife, his children and his grandchildren, Winston slipped away to join the father he had never really known.

Below: Lord Randolph's funeral at Woodstock

For Winston the end of 1894 and the beginning of 1895 was a time of waiting. Waiting on the one hand for the sad but inevitable end to his father's life and on the other for the results of the examinations which would determine the beginning of the next stage of his own life . . . I passed out of Sandhurst into the world. It opened like Aladdin's cave . . . Instead of creeping in at the bottom, almost by charity, I passed with honours . . . I could learn quickly enough the things that mattered . . .

Below: Winston's final results at Sandhurst

											Appointed to a Commission as 2nd Lieutenant.		
	Tactics.	Fortification.	Military Topography.	Drill.	Gymnastics.	Riding.	Musketry.	Marks awarded by Professors.	Total.	Conduct.	Date of Retiring.	Cavalry.	Infantry.	REMARKS.
	278	215	199						1,198	Good, but unpunctual		4ᵗ		
	266	254	207						1,140	Unpunctual				
	263	532	471	95	85	190	105	1,416	2,646	Good	Feb: 95	Hussars 20 Feb 95		
	220	235	172						962	Exemplary				
	207	250	200						961	Exemplary	Feb: 95		Scottish Rifles 6 Mar. 95	
	150	511	392	101	141	121	104	1,145	2,365	Exemplary				
	169	197	203						914	Exemplary				
	215	161	173						875	Good	Feb: 95			Unattached List 216 Jan: 95
	241	475	414	104	140	120	105	1,436	2,319	Very Good				
	179	185	153						897	Exemplary				
	198	248	183						1,007	Exemplary	Feb: 95		Rif. Bde 22-5-95	
	156	471	400	122	122	131	93	380	2,304	Good				
	231	176	185						1,025	Good, but unpunctual			Argyll & Suthd Highrs 20 Feb 95	
	251	216	198						1,089	Very Good	Feb: 95			
	192	497	434	114	130	124	112	1,401	2,430	Exemplary				
	256	228	174						1,074	Exemplary			West India Regt 20 Feb 95	
	241	249	226						1,080	Exemplary	Feb: 95			
	227	558	480	115	105	132	112	540	2,731	Exemplary				
	185	250	253						1,066	Exemplary			N. Riding Regt 28 Sept 95	
	186	231	159						1,025	Exemplary	Aug: 95			
	137	528	360	138	114	170	101	1,440	2,410	Exemplary				
	217	264	206						1,074	Very Good			Roy. Irish Rif. 28 Sept 95	
	227	256	165						1,023	Exemplary	Aug: 95			
	170	534	451	152	154	185	103	1,451	2,619	Very Good				
	199	210	227						1,044	Very Good			Roy. W. Surrey Regt 28 Sept 95	
	190	251	202						982	Very Good	Aug: 95			
	148	527	466	116	156	168	67	424	2,440	Very Good				
	175	281	264						1,061	Very Good				Unattached List 14 Aug 95.
	216	250	186						993	Exemplary	Aug: 95			
	240	500	473	116	134	190	87	537	2,605	Very Good				
	200	217	188						1,050	Good				
	212	247	174						1,075	Very Good	Aug: 95			
	176	508	320	111	107	197	99	533	2,253	Very Good				

Winston had passed his final examinations at Sandhurst, 20th out of 130, a feat which his father would have applauded had he been better able to comprehend what was happening around him.

Once in possession of his results there was the question of which regiment Winston was going to join. He had never intended to join the Infantry and had just gone along with the idea convinced that he would be able to bring his father round to his way of thinking in the end.

Winston records ... After my father's last sad home-coming he could take but little interest in my affairs. My mother explained to him how matters had arranged themselves, and he seemed quite willing, and even pleased, that I should become a Cavalry Officer. Indeed one of the last remarks he made to me was, "Have you got your horses?"

Although no doubt these conversations did take place it is highly unlikely that Lord Randolph was in a fit state to take in their meaning. Knowing that Winston intended to go against his father's wishes, perhaps Lady Randolph wanted to make it easier for him. Winston himself would not have been human if he had not seized on any straw to make his actions, following so soon after Lord Randolph's death, more palatable.

Winston's flirtation with the Cavalry had turned into a love affair when Colonel Brabazon, the commanding officer of the 4th Hussars, invited him while he was at Sandhurst to dine in the regimental Mess . . . **In those days the Mess of a cavalry regiment presented an impressive spectacle to a youthful eye . . . It was like a State banquet . . . having it would seem conducted myself with discretion and modesty, I was invited again on several occasions . . .** When Lady Randolph had raised the subject her husband was emphatically opposed to the idea and wrote . . . *Brabazon, who is I know one of the finest soldiers in the Army, had no business to go and turn that boy's head about going into the 4th Hussars . . .* However, the head was decidedly turned.

There was still the Duke of Cambridge to placate before Winston could give up his place in the 60th

Opposite: Subaltern 4th Hussars

Rifles in favour of the 4th Hussars. Lady Randolph lost no time in approaching the Duke, so that on the 19th February 2nd Lieutenant Churchill wrote to his mother from the 4th Hussars at Aldershot . . . **The work, thought hard and severe is not at present uninteresting, and I trust the novelty & the many compensating attractions of a military existence – will prevent it becoming so – at any rate for the next four or five years** . . . Barely commissioned, he was already looking ahead to a life beyond the military.

In July, Mrs Everest died, her precious Winny at her side. Thus twice within the space of six months Winston came face to face with death, hitherto something he had only envisaged encountering on the battlefield or on a horse, which he thought . . . **taken at a gallop, is a very good death to die.** . . . He had seen the two most important influences on his young life vanish for ever. He had lost the father he adored and respected but never really knew . . . **All my dreams of comradeship with him, of entering Parliament at his side and in his support, were ended. There remained for me only to pursue his aims and vindicate his memory** . . . He had also lost the faithful nurse who had been . . . **my dearest and most intimate friend during the whole of the twenty years I had lived.** . . .

Winston would continue to draw on his mother's wide circle of friends and acquaintances to further his progress through life. Lady Randolph would introduce him to many famous, influential and extremely useful people. But perhaps the most valuable introduction of all had been made when, at the age of twenty, she had entrusted the care of her tiny son to Elizabeth Ann Everest.

Their mutual losses threw Winston and Lady Randolph together as never before . . . **I was now in the main the master of my fortunes. My mother was always at hand to help and advise; but I was now in my 21st year and she never sought to exercise parental control. Indeed she soon became an ardent ally, furthering my plans and guarding my interests with all her influence and boundless energy. She was still at forty young, beautiful and fascinating. We worked together on even terms, more like brother and sister than mother and son. At least so it seemed to me. And so it continued to the end.** . . .

As head of the family Winston found himself burdened with new responsibilities. Lord Randolph's estate would be swallowed by the debts he had left and Lady Randolph's private income would not cover their expenses. His army pay could not establish Winston as the breadwinner of the family or sustain him in any future political career but his audacity and skill with sword and pen were soon to be mobilised and sent into battle.

Above: Mrs Everest's grave in the City of London Cemetery
Opposite: Winston and Lady Randolph . . . On even terms . . .

BIBLIOGRAPHY

Chaplin, E.D.W., *Churchill and Harrow*, Harrow School Bookshop, London, 1941

Churchill, Peregrine and Mitchell, Julian, *Jennie, Lady Randolph Churchill*, Thames Television, London, 1976

Churchill, Randolph, S., *Winston S. Churchill, Volume I: Youth 1974–1900*, Heinemann, London, 1966

Churchill, Winston S., *Lord Randolph Churchill*, Macmillan, London, 1906
My Early Life, Odhams, London, 1930
Painting as a Pastime, Odhams and Ernest Benn, London, 1948

Cornwallis-West, Mrs George, *Reminiscences of Lady Randolph Churchill*, Edward Arnold, London, 1908

Foster, R.F., *Lord Randolph Churchill*, Clarendon Press, Oxford, 1981

Gathorne-Hardy, Jonathan, *The Rise and Fall of the British Nanny*, Weidenfeld & Nicolson, London, 1993 (revised edition)

Leslie, Anita, *The Fabulous Leonard Jerome*, Hutchinson, London, 1954
Jennie, Hutchinson, London, 1969

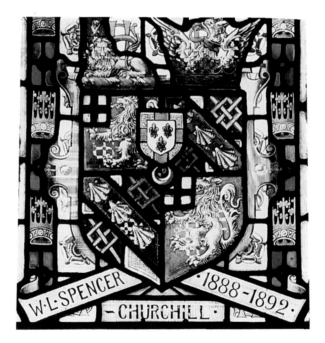